QUIET TALKS ABOUT JESUS

BY
Samuel Dickey Gordon

Dedication

It gives me great pleasure to dedicate this book to Ernie Toppin, a good friend and a talented musician, but oh so much more than that – a faithful minister of God.

Thank you

Parvus Magna Press

5 Ambleside Close, Leyton, London, E10 5RU

Email: sic@pmpress.co.uk

Website: www.pmpress.co.uk

S D Gordon wrote this excellent book in 1906, we have updated the content for the modern reader, replaced anarchism and anglicised the text. If you wish to reprint our version of the text, please just ask!

If you like this edition and you have an idea of another you would like to see please let us know!!

British Library Cataloguing in Publication Data

A catalogue record and a copy of this book are available from the British Library

ISBN: 978-1-910372-13-5 Paperback
ISBN: 978-1-910372-14-2 Paperback
ISBN   978-1-910372-15-9 Kindle/Kobo

Parvus Magna Press publishes limited run and niche interest books in the UK. If you would like to see your book in print, please email your manuscript to sic@pmpress.co.uk

The Evangelical Heritage Library

Welcome to the Evangelical Heritage Library.

There are some books whose impact on the lives of successive generations of Christians deserve to be preserved and distributed as widely as possible.

When I was first approached to edit the Evangelical Heritage Library, I knew for sure the books I wanted to see included and was pleasantly surprised to see them all there on the list.

Some of the books on our list have been out of print for over 100 years and although the odd volume can be found here and there in second hand shops they are mostly lost to the wider public.

The Evangelical Heritage Library format is intended to encourage the reader to study the subjects alongside the author, to this end we have added a couple of extra's to the format of the books.

Wide Outer Margin – we have added the wide margin to allow the reader to mark up and annotate their volume with ease. I have found the issue with studying with antiquated books is that it is close to sacrilege to mark their ancient pages!

We have added, where necessary, footnotes to explain obsolete or archaic text and to give context to references that may be unfamiliar. *In this volume we have also done quite a bit of grammar work as well as replacing US with English spelling of words to try and help the work to flow better for the English reader.*

It is our fervent prayer that this library provides you a route to the throne of God, that there, before His throne, you will get to know Him and the power of His love.

Sharif George
Editor

Free eBook

As part of our commitment to helping you get the most from your Evangelical Heritage Library purchase we are happy to supply a free electronic copy of this book by email or for download from our website.

To claim your free copy of the electronic version of this book, please email sales@pmpress.co.uk with the title of the book you have purchased and where you bought it from and we will send it straight to you.

"Show me, I pray thee, Thy glory." – Moses.

"When I could not see for the glory of that light." – Paul.

"But we all with open face beholding as in a mirror the glory of the Lord are transformed into the same image from glory to glory." – Paul.

"The light of the knowledge of the glory of God in the face of Jesus Christ." – Paul.

"Since mine eyes were fixed on Jesus,
I've lost sight of all beside,
So enchained my spirit's vision,
Looking at the Crucified."
– From Winnowed Hymns.

About S D Gordon

In the early 1900s, S.D. Gordon was a widely travelled speaker in high demand. A prolific author, he wrote more than 25 devotional books, most with the phrase "Quiet Talks" in the title. His first book sold half a million copies over 40 years! He died in 1936.

E.W. Kenyon said that "S.D. Gordon is a sporadic outburst of divine grace. He is unusual, as are all of God's rare tools... he is perfectly balanced in the Word and in the Spirit. He represents that rare but vanishing class of spiritually minded men of the last generation."

"The Treasury of Quiet Talks Selections from S.D. Gordon" (1951) by John W. Bradbury gives this brief biography (adapted): "Samuel Dickey Gordon ministered the deep things of God, he was not an ordained minister, He could boast no academic degrees, he was never doctored [he never received an earned or honorary doctorate]. Theological concepts he obtained from his Bible. A plain man, controlled by a deep desire to edify God's people, he won the respect of the learned and at the same time the affection of the simple.

"Gordon lived a long and useful life. He was born in Philadelphia August 12, 1859 and died June 1936. A public school education was all the academic training he had. But, as a young man, he was hard working, consecrated and sought the best God had for him. He served as assistant secretary of the Philadelphia Young Men's Christian Association in 1884-86 so efficiently that he became state secretary for the YMCA in Ohio, serving from 1886 to 1895. In this period, he developed a quiet style of devotional speaking which was quite the opposite of the powerful forensics which dominated the pulpit style of that period.

"Gordon then took four years to visit the mission fields of the Orient and to tour Europe on speaking missions. His quiet manner, simplicity, illustrative quality and gentle spirit won for him a great following wherever he went. "Quiet Talks on Power" was his first book, published by Fleming H. Revell in 1901. Gordon was then forty-two. His "Quiet Talks on Prayer" followed in 1904, "Quiet Talks on Service" and "Quiet Talks about Jesus", in 1906. The demand for his books had grown so great that he could produce two in a year and follow thereafter with one series of Quiet Talks each year until 1915 when the first World War disrupted everything. After the war he resumed his Quiet Talks in books but not at the same speed. Altogether he produced twenty-five books, twenty-two of which belonged to the Quiet Talks series.

"An incessant and tireless itinerant, Gordon never lacked for opportunities to preach. He never called himself a preacher, preferring the title of lecturer. In a real sense he was unique. His manner of speaking, never dull, always illustrated by parabolic stories, had gripping power to hold the attention and stir the heart."

Peter Wade
www.peterwade.com

Contents

A bit ahead

So far as I can find out, I have no theory about Jesus to make these talks fit into. I have tried to find out for myself what the old Book of God tells about Him. And here I am trying to tell to others, as simply as I can, what I found. It was by the tedious, twisting path of doubt that I climbed the hill of truth up to some of its summits of certainty. I am free to confess that I am ignorant of the subject treated here save for the statements of that Book, and for the assent within my own spirit to these statements, which has greatly deepened the impression they made, and make. There is no question raised here about that Book itself, but simply a taking and grouping up together of what it says.

Most persons simply read a book. A few study it, also. It is good to read. It is yet better to go back over it and study, and meditate. Since learning that the two books on power and prayer have been used in Bible classes I have regretted not including study notes in them. For those who may want to study about Jesus there has been added at the close a simple analysis with references. The reading pages have been kept free of foot-notes to make the reading smooth and easier. The analysis is so arranged that one can quickly turn in reading to the corresponding paragraph or page in the study notes.

A great musician strikes the key-note of a great piece of music, and can skilfully keep it ever sounding its melody through all the changes clear to the end. It has been in my heart to wish that I could do something like that here. If what has come to me has gotten out of me into these pages, there will be found a dominant note of sweetest music – the winsomeness of God in Jesus.

It is in my heart, too, to add this, that I have a friend whose constant presence and prayer have been the atmosphere of this little book in its making.

The purpose of Jesus

The Purpose in Jesus' Coming

God spelling himself out in Jesus.

Jesus is God spelling Himself out in language that man can understand. God and man used to talk together freely. But one-day man went away from God. And then he went farther away. He left home. He left his native land, Eden, where he lived with God. He emigrated from God. And through going away he lost his mother-tongue.

A language always changes away from its native land. Through going away from his native land man lost his native speech. Through not hearing God speak he forgot the sounds of the words. His ears grew dull and then deaf. Through lack of use he lost the power of speaking the old words. His tongue grew thick. It lost its cunning. And so gradually almost all the old meanings were lost.

God has always been eager to get to talking with man again. The silence is hard on Him. He is hungry to be on intimate terms again with his old friend. Of course he had to use a language that man could understand. Jesus is God spelling Himself out so man can understand. He is the A and the Z, and all between, of the Old Eden language of love.

Naturally enough man had a good bit of bother in spelling Jesus out. This Jesus was something quite new. When His life spoke the simple language of Eden again, the human heart with selfishness ingrained said, "That sounds good, but of course He has some selfish scheme behind it all. This purity and simplicity and gentleness can't be genuine." Nobody yet seems to have spelled Him out fully, though they're all trying: All on the spelling bench. That is, all that have heard. Great numbers haven't heard about Him yet. But many, ah! many could get enough, yes, can get enough to bring His purity into their lives and sweet peace into their hearts.

But there were in His days upon earth some sticklers for the old spelling forms. Not the oldest, mind you. Jesus alone stands for that. This Jesus didn't observe the idioms that had grown up outside of Eden. These people had decided that these old forms were the only ones acceptable. And so they disliked Him from the beginning, and quarrelled with Him. These idioms were dearer to them than life – that is, than His life. So having quarrelled, they did worse, and then – softly – worst. But even in their worst, Jesus was God spelling Himself out in the old simple language of Eden. His best came out in their worst.

Some of the great nouns of the Eden tongue – the God tongue – He spelled out big. He spelled out purity, the natural life of Eden; and obedience, the rhythmic harmony of Eden; and peace, the sweet music of Eden; and power, the mastery and dominion of Eden; and love, the throbbing heart of Eden. It was in biggest, brightest letters that love was spelled out. He used the biggest capitals ever known, and traced each in a deep dripping red, with a new spelling – s-a-c-r-i-f-i-c-e.

Jesus is God, following us up.

You see, the heart of God had been breaking – is breaking over the ways things have been going down on this planet. Folk fail to understand Him. Worse yet, they misunderstand Him, and feel free to criticize Him. Nobody has been so much slandered as God. Many are utterly ignorant of Him. Many others who are not ignorant yet ignore Him. They turn their faces and backs. Some give Him the cut direct. The great crowd in every part of the world is yearning after Him: piteously, pathetically, most often speechlessly yearning, blindly groping along, with an intense inner tug after Him. They know the yearning. They feel the inner, upward tug. They don't understand what it is for which they yearn, nor what will satisfy.

For man was made to live in closest touch with God. That is his native air. Out of that air his lungs are badly affected. This other air is too heavy. It's malarial, and full of gases and germy dust. In it he chokes and gasps. Yet he knows not why. He gropes about in the night made by his own shut eyes. He doesn't seem to know enough to open them. And sometimes he will not open them. For the hinge of the eyelid is in the will. And having shut the light out, he gets tangled up in his ideas as to what is light. He puts darkness for light, and light for darkness.

Once man knew God well; close up. And that means loved, gladly, freely. For here to know is to love. But one day a bad choice was made. And the choice made an ugly kink in his will. The whole trouble began there. A man sees through his will. That is his medium for the transmission of light. If it be twisted, his seeing, his understanding, is twisted. The twist in the will regulates the twist in the eye. Both ways, too, for a good change in the will in turn changes the eyes back to seeing straight. He that is willing to do the right shall clearly see the light.

But that first kink seems to have been getting worse kinked ever since. And so man does not see God as He is. Man is cross-eyed Godward, but doesn't know it. Man is colour-blind toward God. The blue of God's truth is to him an arousing, angering red. The soft, soothing green of His love becomes a noisy, irritating yellow. Nobody has been so much misunderstood as God. He has suffered misrepresentation from two quarters: His enemies and His friends. More from – which? Hard to tell. Jesus is God trying to tell men plainly what He is really like.

The world turned down the wrong lane, and has been going that way pell-mell ever since. Yet so close is the wrong lane to the right that a single step will change lanes. Though many results of being in the wrong lane will not be changed by the change of lanes. It takes time to rest up the feet made sore by the roughness of the wrong lane. And some of the scars, where men have measured their length, seem to stay.

The result of that wrong turning has been pitiable. Separation from God, so far as man could make separation. There is no separation on God's part. He has never changed. He remains in the world, but because of man's turning his face away, He remains as a stranger, unrecognized. He remains just where man left Him. And any one going back to that point in the road will find Him standing waiting with an eager light glistening in His eyes. No! That's not accurate. He is a bit nearer than ever He was. He is following us up. He is only a step off. Jesus is God eagerly following us up.

The early Eden picture.

But one will never get to understand this Jesus until he gets a good look at man as he was once, and as he is now. The key to understanding Jesus is man, even as Jesus is the key to God. One must use both keys to get into the inner heart of God. To get hold of that first key one must go back to the start of things. The old Book of God opens with a picture that is fascinating in its simplicity and strength. There is an unfallen man. He is fresh from the hand of God, free of scar and stain and shrivelling influence. He is in a garden. He is walking hand in hand with God, and working side by side with God: friendship and partnership. Friends in spirit: partners in service.

The distinctive thing about the man is that he is like God. He and God are alike. In this he differs from all creation. He is God's link between Himself and His Creation. Particular pains are taken by repetition and change of phrase to make clear and emphatic that it was in the very image of God that man was made. Just what does it mean that we men were made in God's likeness? Well, the thing has been discussed back and forth a good bit. Probably we will not know fully till we know as we are known. In the morning when we see Him we shall be like Him fully again. Then we'll know. That morning's sun will clear up a lot of fog. But a few things can be said about it now with a positive-ness that may clear the air a bit, and help us recognize the dignity of our being, and behave accordingly.

Man came into being by the breath of God. God breathed Himself into man. The breath that God breathed out came into man as life. The very life of man is a bit of God. Man is of the essence of God. Every man is the presence-chamber of God.

God is a Spirit. Man is a spirit. He lives in a body. He thinks through a mind. He is a spirit, using the body as a dwelling-place, and the mind as his keenest instrument. All the immeasurable possibilities and capacities of spirit being are in man.

God is an infinite spirit. That is, we cannot understand Him fully. He is very close to us. The relationship is most intimate, and tender, yet His fullness is ever beyond our grasp and our ken. Man is infinite in that he knows that God is infinite. Only like can appreciate like. He can appreciate that he cannot appreciate God, except in part. He understands that he does not understand God save in smaller part. He knows enough to love passionately. And through loving as well as through knowing he knows that there is infinitely more that he does not know. Only man of all earth's creation knows this. In this he is like God. The difference between God and man here is in the degree of infinity. That degree of difference is an infinite degree. Yet this is the truth. But more yet: man has this same quality towards himself and other men. He is infinite in that he cannot be fully understood in his mental processes and motives. He is beyond grasp fully by his fellow. Even one's most intimate friend who knows most and best must leave unknown more than is known.

God is an eternal spirit. He has always lived. He will live always. He knows no end, at either end. All time before there was time, and after the time-book is shut, is to Him a passing present. Man is an eternal spirit, because of God. He will know no end. He will live always because the breath of God is his very being.

God is love. He yearns for love. He loves. And more, He is love. Man is like God in his yearning for love, in his capacity for love, and in his lovableness. Man must love. He lives only as he loves. True love, and only that, is the real life. He will give up everything for love. He is satisfied only as he loves and finds love. To love is greater than to be loved. One cannot always have both. God does not. But every one may love. Everyone does love. And only as there is love, pure and true – however overlaid with what is not so – only so is there life.

God is holy. That word seems to include purity and righteousness. There is utter absence of all that should not be. There is in Him all that should be, and that in fullness beyond our thinking. Man was made holy. There is in the Genesis picture of Eden a touch that for simplicity and yet for revealing the whole swing of moral action is most vivid. In the presence of conditions where man commonly, universally, the world around, and time through, has been and is most sensitive to suggestion of evil there is with this first man the utter absence of any thought of evil.[1] In the light of after history there could be no subtler, stronger statement than this of his holiness, his purity, at this stage.

And in his capacity for holiness, in that intensest longing for purity, and loathing of all else, that comes as the Spirit of God is allowed sway, is revealed again the capacity for God-likeness. It is the prophetic dawn within of that coming Eden when again we shall see His face, and have the original likeness fully restored.

God is wise, all-wise. Among the finest passages of the' Christian's classic are those that represent God as personified wisdom. And here wisdom includes all knowledge and justice. That the Spirit of God breathed into man His own mental life is stated most keenly by the man who proverbially embodied in himself this quality of wisdom. "The spirit of man is the lamp of the Lord searching out the innermost parts." The allusion is clearly to intellectual powers. There is in man the same quality of mental keenness that searches into things as is in God. It is often dulled, gripped by a sort of stupor, so overlaid you would hardly guess it was there. But, too, as we all know, it often shines out with a startling brilliance. It is less in degree than with God, but it is the same thing, a bit of God in man. This explains man's marvellous achievements in literature, in invention, in science, and in organization.

Two light master-strokes of the etching point in the Eden picture reveal the whole mental equipment of the man. The only sayings of Adam's preserved for us are when God brought to him the woman. She is the occasion for sayings that reveal the mental powers of this first man. Fittingly it is so. Woman, when true to herself, has ever been the occasion for bringing out the best in man. "And the man said, this time it is bone of my bones, and flesh of my flesh; this shall be called woman, because out of man was this one taken. Therefore, doth a man leave his father and his mother and cleave unto his wife, and they become one flesh." ... "And the man called his wife's name Eve; because she was the mother of all living." Here is revealed at a glance the keen mental powers at work. Here is the simplicity of statement that marks the speech of strong men. The whole forest is in a single acorn. The whole of a human life is in the primal cell. The chemist knows the whole body by looking into one drop of blood. Here is revealed in one glance the whole man. Mark the keen sense of fitness in the naming of woman – the last and highest creation. Adam was a philologist. His mind was analytical. Inferentially the same keen sense of fitness guided in all the names he had chosen. Here is recognition of the plan for the whole race, a simple unlaboured foresight into its growth. A man's relation to his wife, his God-chosen friend, as being the closest of life, and above all others is recognized, together with the consequent obligation upon him. She comes first of all. She becomes the first of all his relationships. The man and the woman – one man and one woman – united, make the true unit of society. Any disturbance of that strikes at the very vitals of society.

And God is a Sovereign – the sovereign of the vast swing of worlds. Man likewise is a sovereign in the realm of nature, and over all the lower creation. He was given dominion, kingship, over all the earth-creation. Man is a king. He is of the blood royal. He was made to command, to administrate, to reign. He is the judge of last appeals on the bench of earth.

But there is more here. The chief characteristic of an absolute sovereign is the imperial power to choose, to decide. Man was made an absolute sovereign in his own will. God is the absolute sovereign. He has made man an absolute sovereign in one realm, that of his will, his power of choice. There is one place where man reigns alone, an absolute autocrat, where not even God can come save as the autocrat desires it, that is in his will. And if that "can" bother you, remember that it was God's sovereign act that made it so. So that God remains sovereign in making man a sovereign in the realm of his will. There every man sits in imperial solitude.

Here then is the picture of man fresh from the hand of God. A spirit, in a body, with an unending life, partly infinite, like God in his capacity for love, for holiness, and wisdom, with the gift of sovereignty over the lower creation, and in his own will. Like Him too in his capacity for fellowship with God. For only like can have fellowship with like. It is only in that in which we are alike that we can have fellowship. These two, God and man, walking side by side, working together, friendship in spirit; partnership in service.

This man is in a garden of trees and bushes, with fruit and flowers and singing birds, roses with no pricking thorns, soft green with no weeds, and no poison ivy, for there is no hate. And he is walking with God, talking familiarly as chosen friend with choicest friend. Together they work in the completion of creation. God brings His created beings one by one to man to be catalogued and named, and accepts his decisions. What a winsome picture. These two, God and a man in His likeness, walking and working side by side; likeness in being; friendship, fellowship in spirit; partnership, comradeship in service. And this is God's thought for man!

Man's bad break.

Then come the climax and the crisis. A climax is the climbing to the top rung of the ladder. A crisis is the meeting place of possible victory and possible disaster. A single step divides between the two – the precipice-height, and the canon's yawning gulf.

It was a climax of opportunity; and a crisis of action. God's climax of opportunity to man. Man's crisis of action. God made man sovereign in his power of choice. Now He would go the last step and give him the opportunity of using that power and so reaching the topmost levels. God led man to the hill of choice. The man must climb the hill if he would reach its top.

Only the use of power gives actual possession of the power. What we do not use we lose. The pressure of the foot is always necessary to a clear title. To him that hath possible power shall be given actual power through use.

This opportunity was the last love-touch of God in opening up the way into the fullness of His image. With His ideal for man God went to His limit in giving the power. He could give the power of choice. Man must use the power given. Only so could he own what had been given. God could open the door. Man must step over the door-sill. Action realizes power.

The tree of knowledge of good and evil was the tree of choice. Obedience to God was the one thing involved. That simply meant, as it always means, keeping in warm touch with God. All good absolutely is bound up in this – obeying God, keeping in warm touch. To obey Him is the very heart of good. All evil is included in disobeying Him. To disobey, to fail to obey is the seeded core of all evil.

Whichever way he chose he would exercise his God-like power of choice. Whichever way he chose; the knowledge would come. If he chose to obey he would know good by choosing it, and evil by rejecting it. He knew neither good nor evil, for he had not yet had the contact of choice. Knowledge comes only through experience. In choosing not to obey, choosing to disobey, he would know evil with a bitter intimacy by choosing it. He would become acquainted with the good which he had shoved ruthlessly away.

With the opportunity came the temptation: God's opportunity; Satan's temptation. Satan is ever on the heels of God. Two inclined planes lead out of every man's path. Two doors open into them side by side. God's door up, the tempter's door down, and only a door-jamb between. Here the split hoof can be seen sticking from under the cloak's edge at the very start. Satan hates the truth. He is afraid of it. Yet he sneaks around the sheltering corner of what he fears and hates. The sugar coating of his gall pills he steals from God. The devil bare-faced, standing only on his own feet, would be instantly booted out at first approach. And right well he knows it.

A cunning half lie opens the way to a full-fledged lie, but still coupled with a half-truth. The suggestion that God was harshly prohibiting something that was needful leads to the further suggestion that He was arbitrarily, selfishly holding back the highest thing, the very thing He was supposed to be giving, that is, likeness to Himself. Eve was getting a course in suggestion. This was the first lesson. The school seems to be in session still. The whole purpose is to slander God, to misrepresent Him. That has been Satan's favourite method ever since. God is not good. He makes cruel prohibitions. He keeps from us what we should have. It is passing strange how every one of us has had that dust in his eyes. Some of us might leave the "had" out of that sentence.

See how cunningly the truth and the lie are interwoven by this old past-master in the sooty art of lying. "Your eyes shall be opened, and ye shall be as God knowing good and evil." It was true because by the use of this highest power of choice he would become like God, and through choosing he would know. It is cunningly implied with a sticky, slimy cunning that, by not eating, that likeness and knowledge would not come. That was the lie. The choice either way would bring both this element of likeness to God in the sovereign power of choice, and the knowledge.

Then came the choice. The step up was a step down: up into the use of his highest power; down by the use of that power. In that wherein he was most like God in power, man became most unlike God in character. First the woman chose: then the man. Satan subtly begins his attack upon the woman. Because she was the weaker? Certainly not. Because she was the stronger. Not the leader in action, but the stronger in influence. He is the leader in action: she in influence. The greater includes the less. Satan is a master strategist, bold in his cunning. If the citadel can be gotten, all is won. If he could get the woman, he would get the man. She includes him. She who was included in him now includes him. The last has become first.

She was deceived. He was not deceived. The woman chose unwarily for the supposed good. The man chose with open eyes for the woman's sake. Could the word gallantry be used? Was it supposed friendship? He would not abandon her? Yet he proved not her friend that day, in stepping down to this new low level. Man's habit of giving smoothly spoken words to woman, while shying sharp-edged stones at her, should in all honesty be stopped. Man can throw no stones at woman. If the woman failed God that day, the man failed both God and the woman. If it be true that through her came the beginning of the world's sin, through her, too, be it gratefully and reverently remembered, came that which was far greater – the world's Saviour.

The choice was made. The act was done. Tremendous act! Bring your microscope and peer with awe into that single act. No fathoming line can sound its depth. No measuring rod its height nor breadth. No thought can pierce its intensity. That reaching arm went around a world. Millenniums in a moment. A million miles in a step. An ocean in a drop. Volumes in a word. A race in a woman. A hell of suffering in an act. The depths of woe in a glance. The first chapter of Romans in

Genesis three, six. Sharpest pain in softest touch. God mistrusted – distrusted. Satan embraced. Sin's door open. Eden's gate shut.

Mark keenly the immediate result that came with that intense rapidity possible only to mental powers. At once they were both conscious of something that had not entered their thoughts before. To the pure all things are pure. To the imagination hurt by breaking away from God, the purest things can bring up suggestions directly opposite. Through the open door of disobedience came with lightning swiftness the suggestion of using a pure, holy function of the body in a way and for a purpose not intended. Making an end of that which was meant to be only a means to a highest end. Degrading to an animal pleasure that which held in its pure hallowed power the whole future of the race. There is absolutely no change save in the inner thought. But what a horrid heredity in that one flash of the imagination! Every sin lives first in the imagination. The imagination is sin's brooding and birth-place. An inner picture, a lingering glance, a wrong desire, an act – that is the story of every sin. The first step was disobedience. That opened the door. The first suggestion of wrong-doing that followed hot on the heels of that first step, through that open door, struck at the very vitals of the race – both its existence and its character. That first suggested unnatural action, with its whole brood, has become the commonest and slimiest sin of the race.

Here, in the beginning, the very thought shocked them. In that lay their safety. Shame is the recoil of God's image from the touch of sin. Shame is sin's first checkmate. It is man's vantage for a fresh pull up. There are only two places where there is no shame: where there is no sin; where sin is steeped deepest in. The extremes are always jostling elbows. Instantly the sense of shame suggested a help. A simple bit of clothing was provided. It was so adjusted as to help most. Clothing is man's badge of shame. The first clothing was not for the body, but for the mind. Not for protection, but for concealment, that so the mind might be helped to forget its evil suggestions. It is one of sin's odd perversions that draws attention by colour and cut to the race's badge of shame. It would seem strongly suggestive of moral degeneracy, or of bad taste, or, let us say in charity, of a lapse of historical memory.

Mark the sad soliloquy of God: "Behold the man has become as one of us: He has exercised his power of choice." He tenderly refrains from saying, "and has chosen wrong! so pitiably wrong!" That was plain enough. He would not rub in the acid truth. He would not make the scar more hideous by pointing it out. "And now lest he put forth his hand

and take of the tree of life." "Lest!" There is a further danger threatening. In his present condition he needs guarding for his own sake in the future. "Lest" – wrong choice limits future action. Sin narrows.

With man's act of sin came God's act of saving. Satan is ever on the heels of God to hurt man. But God is ever on the heels of Satan to cushion the hurt and save the man. It is a nip-and-tuck race with God a head and a heart in the lead. Something had to be done. Man had started sin in himself by his choice. The taint of disobedience, rebellion, had been breathed out into the air. He had gotten out of sorts with his surroundings. His presence would spoil his own heaven. The stain of his sin would have been upon his eternal life. The zero of selfishness would have been the atmosphere of his home. The touch of his unhallowed hand must be taken away for his own sake. That unhallowed touch has been upon every function and relationship of life outside those gates. Nothing has escaped the slimy contact.

Sin could not be allowed to stay there. Its presence stole heaven away from heaven. Yet sin had become a part of the man. The man and the wrong were interwoven. They were inseparable. Sin has such a tenacious, gluey, sticky touch! Each included the other. It could not be put out without his being put out. So man had to be driven out for his own sake to rid his home-spot of sin. The man was driven out that he might come back – changed. Love drove him out that later it might let him in. The tree of life was kept from him for a time that it might be kept for him for an eternity.

When he had changed his spirit, and changed sides in the fight with evil started that day, and gotten victory over the spirit now dominant within himself, those gates would swing again. When the stain of his choice would be taken out of his fibre it would be his right eagerly to retrace these forced steps, and the coming back would find more than had been left. Love has been busy planning the home-coming. The tree of life has been grown in his absence to a grove of trees. The life has become life more abundant.

Outside the Eden gate.

The story of what took place outside that guarded gate makes clear the love, the wise farsighted love that showed the man the way out that day. To tell the story one must use a pen made of the iron that has entered his own soul, and though the pen be eased with ball point, it scratches and sticks in the paper for sheer reluctance. And only the tears of the heart will do for ink.

That was a costly meal. That first bite must have been a big one. Its taste is still in the mouth of the race. If that fruit were an apple it must have been a crab. There has been a bad case of indigestion ever since. If you think there were no crab-apples in Eden, then the touch of those thickening lips must have soured it in the eating – man's teeth are still on edge. The fruit became tough in the chewing. It's not digested yet. That Garden of Eden must have been on a hill, with lowlands below, and high hills above, and roads both ways. The man seems to have gotten into the lowland road, and after a bit, struck some marshes and swamps, with a good bit of thick grey fog.

The first result of the break with God was in the man himself. Man has two doors opening into himself from God – the eye and the ear. Through these God comes into the man and makes Himself known. Through these comes all man knows of God. Both have their hinges in the will, the heart. Man gave both doors a slam shut that day in Eden. Yet they went shut gradually. That was the God-side of their shutting. He quickly slipped in an air cushion so the shutting might be softened and delayed, and meanwhile His presence be appealing to the man.

Refusing to obey God was equal to hearing without being willing to listen. It was the same thing as looking with that reluctance that won't see, and then doesn't see. Hearing and seeing lie deeper than ears and eyes, down in the purpose, the will, the desire of the heart. Unwillingness dulls, and then deafens the ears. It blurs, and then blinds the eye. An earnest, loving purpose gives peculiar keenness to the ears, and opens the eye of the eye. Ears and eyes are very sensitive organs. If their messages be not faithfully attended to they sulk and pout and refuse to transmit messages. It is a remarkable fact that habitual inattention to a sound or sight makes one practically deaf or blind to it; and that close attention persisted in makes one's ears and eyes almost abnormally keen and quick. Love's ears and eyes are proverbially acute.

One may be so wholly absorbed in something that he absolutely does not see the thing on which his eyes are turned. He does not hear the sounds that are plainly coming to his ear because his thought, back of that his heart, is elsewhere. Hearing, seeing is with the heart back of ears and eyes. God is spoken of as silent. Yet His silence may be simply our deafness. The truth is He is speaking all the time, but we are so absorbed that we do not hear. He is ever looking into our faces with His great, tender, deep eyes, but we are so wrapped up in something else that the gaze out of our eyes is vacant to that Face, and with keenest disappointment, so often repeated, He gets no answering glance.

Let anybody in doubt about the strict accuracy of this do some experimenting on himself, either with outer things or regarding God. Let him obey the inner voice in some particular that may perhaps cut straight across some fixed habit, and then watch very quietly for the result. It will come with surprising sureness and quickness. And the reason why is simple. The man is simply moving back into his native air, and of course all the powers work better.

This truth about the nerves of the ears and eyes running down into the heart is constantly being sounded out in the old Book. A famous bit in Isaiah puts it very clearly, and becomes a sort of pivot passage of all others of this sort. That fine-grained, intense-spirited young Hebrew was caught in the temple one day by a sight of God. That wondrous sight held him with unyielding grip through all the after years. With the sight came the voice, and the message for the nation: "Tell these people – you are continually hearing, but you do not listen, nor take in what you hear. Your eyes are open, they look, but they do not see." Then the voice said, "Make their heart fat, and their ears heavy, and their eyes shut."

That is to say, by continually telling them what they will continually refuse to hear because it does not suit the habit of their lives, he would be setting in motion the action that would bring these results. The ears that won't hear by and by can't hear. The heart that will not love and obey gets into a state of fatty degeneration. The valves that refuse to move in loving obedience will get too heavy with fat to move at all. The fat clogs the hinges. There is the touch of a soft irony in the form of the message. As though Isaiah's talking would affect their ears, whereas it is their refusal to hear that stupefies the hearing organ. In faithfulness God insists on telling them the truth even though He knows that their refusal to do will make things worse. But then God is never held back from good by the possible bad that may work out of it.

When Jesus came, the Jews, to whom His messages to the world were directly spoken, were in almost the last stages of that sort of thing. So Jesus, with the fine faithfulness of love blending with the keenest tact, spoke in language veiled by parable to overcome the intense prejudice against plainly spoken truth. They were so set against what He had to tell that the only way to get anything into them at all was so to veil its form as to befool them into thinking it truer. Toward the close, His keenness, for which they were no match, joining with the growing keenness of their hate, made them see at once that the sharp edge of some of those last parables was turned toward themselves.

In explaining to His puzzled disciples about this form of teaching, with a sad irony that reveals both His heart's yearning and His mental keenness, He uses more than once with variations this famous bit from Isaiah. He makes the truth stand out more sharply by stating the opposite of what He desires, making the contrast between His words and His known desires so strong as not only to make plain the meaning intended, but to give it a sharper emphasis.

The result that began with ears and eyes quickly affected the tongue. That is nature's path. The inner road from ear and eye is straight to the tongue. The tongue is the index of man's whole being. While through ear and eye he receives all that ever gets in, through the tongue his whole being is revealed. Of course his personality reveals itself very much otherwise. In the carriage of the body. Strikingly so in the look of the eye. The body itself, especially the face, becomes in time the mould of the spirit within. Yet the tongue – what is said, how it is said, what is not said, the tone of voice – the tongue is the index of the spirit.

There is no stronger indication of mastery over one's powers than in control of the tongue. When God would break up man's first great ambitious scheme of a self-centred monopoly on the Shinar plains, He simply touched his tongue. The first evidence of God's touch in the re-making of man on that memorable Pentecost day was upon his tongue.

The effect upon his tongue of the break with God has been radical and strange. Dumbness, and slowness or thickness of speech alternate with an unnatural sharpness. Sometimes the spittle has a peculiar oiliness that results in a certain slipperiness of statement. Sometimes it has a bitter, poisonous, acid quality that eats its way into the words. There is a queer backward movement in biting sometimes. Withal a strange looseness of speech regarding the holiest things, and the most awesome truths, and the Holy One Himself.

The moment a man gets a vision of God he is instantly conscious of something the matter with his tongue. The sight that comes to his eyes, the sound to his ears makes him painfully self-conscious regarding the defect in his tongue. Moses found himself slow-tongued. Isaiah felt the need of the cleansing coal for his tongue.

But man's whole inner mental process was affected. A peculiar sense of fear, of dread, is woven inextricably into the very fibre of man's being.

His first reported word after that break was, "I was afraid." That sense of fear – a horrid, haunting, nightmare thing – has affected all his thinking and planning and every-day speech. No phrase is oftener on man's tongue than "I'm afraid." Isaiah's classic utterance about ears and eyes has a counterpart equally classic from Paul's pen, about the effect of sin upon man's mental processes. A few lines in the letter to the Ephesian circle of churches give a sort of bill of details of the mental steps down that slope from the Eden gate.

Paul is urging these friends to live no longer as they, in common with all the races, had been living, in "the vanity of their mind, being darkened in their understanding, alienated from the life of God, because of the ignorance that is in them, because of the hardening of their hearts; who, being past feeling, gave themselves up to lasciviousness to make a greedy trade of all uncleanness." Here are seven steps down. The first five are put in reverse order. Beginning where they have been, he traces the five steps back to the starting point, and then adds the two likely to follow with any who persist past this point.

The start of all sin is in the setting of one's self against God. Choosing some other way than His. It is called here "hardening of the heart." The native juices of the heart are drawn away from God and dry up. In this Book the heart is the seat of both affection and will. It is the pivotal organ of life. Any trouble there quickly and surely affects the whole being. Then follows "ignorance." Of course. The heart controls both ear and eye, the two great channels inward of knowledge. The hardening of the heart locks both doors. And hard on the heels of that comes "Alienated from the life of God." That is, cut off, shut out of fellowship and intimacy. Life is union with God. Through union God's life flows into us. Union is rooted in knowledge and in sympathy, fellow-feeling, a common desire and purpose. The man snapping that tying cord cuts himself off.

The next step is peculiarly pathetic – "darkened in their understanding." The man has shut the shutters close, and pulled the shades down tight. Of course it's dark inside. He is unable to see. First unwilling, now unable. If the only thing that can be gotten for use as light be darkness, how intense is that darkness! Then comes the pitiable result of acting as if darkness were man's native air – "the vanity of the mind." That word vanity means aimlessness. The mind is still keen, even brilliant, but the guiding star is shut out, and that keen mind goes whirring aimlessly around. Sometimes a very earnest aimlessness. The man is on a foggy sea without sun or star. The compass on board is useless.

But more pitiable and pathetic yet; indeed, utterly laughable if it were not so terribly serious and pathetic: - this man in the dark proceeds gravely to decide that this darkness of his own making is a superior sort of light, and bows low in worship of its maker. He has even been known to write brilliant essays on the light-giving power of blinding darkness, with earnest protests at the evil of this thing commonly called light. Sometimes having carefully cottoned up the shutters that no scrap of sun light or sun warmth may get in, he strikes a friction match, and sits warming himself, and eloquently sets forth his own greatness as shown by the match, friction match. Most of this sort of light and heat is of the friction sort.

Then with reluctant hand, one who knows Paul's tender heart can well believe, the curtain is drawn aside for the last two stages; the grosser, gutter, animal stages, which, not always by any means, but all too commonly follow. "Past feeling!" The delicate sense of feeling about right and purity dulls and goes. The fine inner judgment blunts and leaves. The shrinking sensitiveness toward the dishonourable and impure loses its edge and departs. Then —pell-mell, like a pack of dogs down a steep hill, follows the last "lasciviousness," the purest, holiest things in the gutter-slime, and then, cold-blooded, greedy trading in these things. That's the picture painted in shadows of Rembrandt blackness, newly blackened, of the effect in man himself of turning away from God.

Now Jesus is the music of God's heart sounding in man's ears anew, that he may be wooed back the old road to the Eden life. Jesus is the face of God, close up, looking tenderly, yearningly, into man's face, that his eye may be caught and held, and his heart be enchained.

Sin's brood.

The second great result of that Eden break has been in the growth of sin. In the seventeenth century after that it was said that man's heart was a breeding place of thoughts whose pictured forms were bad, only bad, with no spots of good, nor spurts of good. A thousand years later, Moses giving the Hebrew tribes the ten commandments, adds a crowd of particulars, some of them very gruesome, which serve as mirrors to reveal the common practice of his age. The slant down of those first centuries has evidently been increasing in its downward pitch.

More than a thousand years later yet, there is a summary made by Paul that reveals the stage reached by sin in his day. Probably no one knew the world of his time, which has proved to be the world's crisis time, as did Paul the scholar and philosopher of Tarsus. Himself a city man, well-bred and well-schooled, a world traveller, with acute, disciplined powers of observation, and a calm scholarly judgment, he had studied every phase of life cultured and lowly.

He pitched upon the great city centres in his active campaigning, and worked out into the country districts. He was a world-bred man. He knew the three over-lapping worlds of his time: The Hebrew, with its ideals of purity and religion; the Greek, with its ideals of culture; and the Roman, with its ideals of organization and conquest. He is writing from Corinth, then the centre of Greek life, to Rome, the centre of the world's life. His letter is the most elaborate of any of his writings preserved to us. In its beginning he speaks of man, universally, morally, as he had come to know him. His arraignment is simply terrific in its sweep and detail.

Let me pause and be measuring the words cautiously and then put this down: - the description of the latter half of the first chapter of Romans is a true description of man to-day. At first flush that sounds shocking, as indeed it is. It seems as if this description can apply only to degraded savages and to earth's darkest corners. But the history of Paul's day, and before, and since, and an under view of the social fabric to-day, only serve to make clear that Paul's description is true for all time, and around the world.

There is a cloak of conventionality thrown over the blacker tints of the picture to-day in advanced Christian lands. It is considered proper to avoid speaking of certain excesses, or, if speech must be used, modestly to say "un-nameable." And it is a distinct gain for morality that it is so. Better a standard recognized, even though broken. But commonly the conditions are not changed. The differences found in different civilizations to-day are differences only of degree. In the most advanced cities of Christendom to-day may be found every bit of this chapter's awful details, but properly cloaked. In European lands the cloaks are sewed with the legal-stitch, which is considered the proper finish. In lands where our Christian standards are not recognized the thing is as open as in this chapter.

In four short paragraphs containing sixty-six lines in the American Revision, Paul packs in his terrific philippic[1]. He swings over the ground four times. Nowhere does he reveal better his own fidelity to truth, with the fineness of his own spirit. Here, delicacy of expression is rarely blended with great plainness. No one can fail to understand, and yet

---

[1] Philippic – a bitter attack or denunciation, especially a verbal one.

that sense of modesty native to both man and woman is not improperly disturbed, even though the recital be shocking.

Here is paragraph one: Man knew God both through nature and by the direct inner light. But he did not want Him as God. It bothered the way he wanted to live. The core of all sin is there. All its fruitage grows about that core. He became vain in his reasoning. He gave himself up to keen, brilliant speculation. Having cut the cord that bound him to God, unanchored, without compass, on a shoreless, starless sea, he drifts brilliantly about in the dense grey fog.

Then he fooled himself further by thinking himself wise. He preferred somebody else to God. Whom? Himself! Then – birds; then-beasts on all fours with backbone on a line with the earth, nose and mouth close to the ground; then – grey-black, slimy, crawling, creeping things. He traded off the truth of God for a lie; the sweet purity of God for rank impurity. He dethroned God, and took the seat himself. He bartered God for beasts and grew like that he preferred. God's gracious restraint is withdrawn when he gets down to the animal stage. Only here man out-animalled the animals. The beasts are given points on beastliness. The life he chose to live held down by the throat the truth he knew so well. That's the first summary.

The next two paragraphs are devoted to that particular sort of unnatural sin first suggested to man after his disobedience, and which in all time and all lands has been and is the worst, the most unnatural, the most degrading, and the most common. It came first in the imagination. It came early in the history of actual sin. It is put first by Paul in his arraignment here. He gives it chief place by position and by particularity of description. First was the using of a pure, natural function to gratify unnatural desires. Then with strange cunning and lustful ingenuity changing the natural functions to uses not in the plan of nature. Let it all be said in lowest, softest voice, so sadly awful is the recital. Yet let that soft voice be very distinct, that the truth may be known. Then lower down yet the commercializing of such things. Unconcerned barter and trade in man's holy, most potent function. Putting highest price on most ingenious impurity.

Then follows the longest of these paragraphs running up and down the grimy gamut of sin. Beginning with all unrighteousness, he goes on to specify depravity, greedy covetousness, maliciousness. Oozing out of every pore there are envy, murder, strife, deceit, malignity. Men are whisperers, backbiters, God-haters, and self-lovers, in that they are insolent, haughty, boastful. They are inventors of evil things, without understanding, breakers of faith, without natural affection, ruthlessly merciless.

The climax is reached in this, that though they know God, and what He has set as the right rule of life, they not only do these things named, but they delight in the fellowship of those who habitually practise them. The stage of impulsiveness is wholly gone. They have settled down to this as the deliberate choice and habit of life. Man is still a king, but all bemired. He is the image and glory of God, but how shrivelled and withered; obscured, all overgrown with ugly poison vines.

Let it be remembered at once that this is a composite picture of the race. Many different sorts of men must be put together to get such a view. Sin works out differently in different persons. A man's activities take on the tinge of his personality. So sin in a man takes on the colour and tone of his individuality.

One man has the inner disposition against God, accompanied by no excesses at all. These things disgust him. He is refined in his tastes, perhaps scholarly and intellectual in his thinking. That inner disposition may be a sort of refined ignoring of God either defiant or indifferent. In another, the animal nature swings to the front, stronger perhaps by heredity, and, yielded to, it runs to the excess of riot. Then there is the man with the strange yellow fever, whose love for the bright-coloured precious metal burns in his blood and controls every impulse and purpose. And the man with intense love of power, of controlling men and things for the sake of the immense power involved, with himself as the centre of all.

There is every imaginable degree of each of these, and every sort of combination among them. The lines cross and re-cross at every possible angle in various persons. A man is apt to get money-drunk then society-drunk (with a special definition for the word society in this connection), then lust-drunk. Or, he may swing direct from money-intoxication into power-intoxication. Please notice keenly that each of these four grows up out of a perfectly normal, natural desire. Sin always follows nature's grooves. There is nothing wrong in itself. The sin is in the wrong motive underneath, or the wrong relationship round about an act. Or, it is in excess, exaggeration, pushing an act out of its true proportion. Exaggeration floods the stream out of its channel. Wrong motive or wrong relationship sends a bad stream into a good channel.

But sift down under the surface and always is found the same thing. The upper growth is varied by what it finds on the surface to mingle with, but the sub-stuff is ever the same. The root always is self. The whole seed of sin is in preferring one's own way to God's way; one's self to God. The stream of life is turned the wrong way. It is turned in. Its true direction is up. The true centre of gravity for man is not downward, nor inward, but upward and outward.

God's treatment of sin.

God's treatment of sin lets in a flood of light on the sort of thing it is. Three times over in this summary Paul says that God "gave them up." As they cast out all acknowledgment of God, He gave them up to an outcast mind. When they turned God out-of-doors, God left them indoors to themselves. It was the worst thing He could do, and the best. Worst – to be left alone with sin. Best, because the sin would get so vile that the man in God's image would want to turn it out, and get God back. Man never turns from sin until he feels its vileness to the sickening point. When things get to the acute stage, and a sharp crisis is on, then as a rule there will be an eager turning to the One who can cleanse and make over new; but usually not until then.

Sin has a terrific gait. Give it a loose rein and man will get winded and ready to drop. Only then is he ready to drop it. Sin can't be patched up or mended. Nursing only helps it to its feet for a fresh start. The whole trouble is in the nature of the thing. The heart pumps the hot blood of rebellion. Its lungs can breathe only self-willed air. The worst punishment of sin is that left alone it breeds more sin, and worse sin. The worst of sin is in its brood. It is very prolific. Every sin is a seed-sin. The breeding process gets the sort more refined in its coarseness.

'This is the very curse of evil deed,
That of new sin it becomes the seed.'[2]

And the plain statements of the Book, and the inevitable working of man's nature, reveal all the bad results of sin intensifying indefinitely in the after-life. Jesus is God letting sin do its worst, upon Himself, that man might see its utter, stubborn damnableness, and eagerly turn from it, and back to Him.

---

[2] Schiller (original footnote)

A bright gleam of light.

Yet be it keenly marked, there is a very bright gleam of light across this dark picture. In going over the story of sin with its terrific results now and afterward, one needs to be very tender, for he is talking about men – his brothers. And to be very careful not to say things that are not so. Some good, earnest people have been thinking that the whole race except a small minority were given over to eternal misery. The vast majority of men has never heard the name of Jesus. And some very godly people have seemed to think that these are lost forever.

Yet the old Book of God speaks very plainly here. Its meaning can be gotten without any twisting of words. Neither the Jewish nation nor the Christian Church can be regarded as favourites of God. God has no favourites for salvation. The Jewish nation was chosen for service' sake. Through it there came a special after-revelation of God. Through it came the world's new Man. The Church is the repository of God's truth to-day, with its window panes not always quite clear. Its great mission is to tell the whole race of Jesus. Both were chosen for service.

Every nation knew God directly at the first. And be it said thoughtfully, every man has enough of revelation and of inner light to lead him back to God. A man's choice in this life is his choice always. Any student of the ordinary working of man's mind can certify that. Whatever sort of being a man deliberately, persistently chooses to be here and now, he will be always. The only change possible in the after-life will be in the degree. Never in the sort.

The Gospels speak of believing on Jesus, and of the bad results for those who decline or refuse to have anything to do with Him. Of course it is speaking of those who have heard of Him. There can be no believing on Jesus without hearing, and of course in simple fairness no condemning on any such grounds. The gospel message is wholly concerned with those who hear.

But there is clear and plain teaching about the great outside majority of past generations and of our own who have never heard. It was a member of both Jewish nation and Christian Church, whose tongue, touched by the Spirit of God, said, "God is no respecter of persons: but in every nation he that feareth Him and worketh righteousness is acceptable to Him." That is a simple standard, yet a searching one. Anybody, anywhere, with a truly reverential thought upward, and a controlling purpose to be right in his life, will find the door swinging wide. No other badges or tickets required. This would include that remarkable woman of India, Chundra Lelah[3], all those weary years before the simple story of Jesus brought its flood of light and peace, and all of her innumerable class.

Paul puts it as simply and a little more fully in the letter to the Romans, that careful treatise which sums up with marvellous fullness and brevity the gospel he preached to the world. In chapter two, he says, "to them who by patience in well-doing seek for glory and honour and incorruption (He will give) eternal life." Note that in his review thus far he has not yet gotten to Jesus the Saviour.

These people of whom he is now speaking have never heard of Jesus. They are the great majority. Mark keenly the simple description of them. It is a description, not of an achievement, but of a purpose. The absorbing aim in their lives is seeking upward. The seeking controls the life. The mastering spirit of these seekers is patience, steadfastness. They are seeking for the highest thing. They are doing what seems to them to be right, while seeking. They are doing right patiently.

Patience! What a world of conflicting experiences in a word! Misunderstandings, breaks, slips, stumbling, failures, falls; but in all, through all, patience, steadfastness. Taking a fresh hold at every turn. And the gripping fingers ever learning a new tenacity. Pulling steadily up a steep mountain side, in a blazing hot sun, blinded by dust, struck by loosened rocks above rolling down, but – patiently, steadily, with dust-blinded eyes, tugging up. To such is given the heart's desire – eternal life. Ah! God judges a man by his direction, by the set of his face. He may not be far up, but his face is turned up. His heels show their backs. His toes point toward the top. That reveals the purpose, the desire of the man inside. His choice is to be up. And it is choice that makes character as well as revealing it. And the one thing that concerns God is the character as revealed in the purpose.

There is a simple, pathetic story from mission lands, variously told, and well vouched for, of a missionary pausing long enough in a village to tell the story of Jesus to the crowd that gathered, and then pushing on. This was the first visit of a missionary to this place and so the first news of Jesus. The crowd listened eagerly with various results. There was one listener, an old man, held in repute for his wisdom, who at once accepted the missionary's story, and announced his acceptance of Jesus. His neighbours expressed their surprise at his prompt acceptance of such a new thing. The old man's quiet answer in effect was this: "Oh, I

---

[3] "An Indian Priestess." Published by Hodder & Stoughton.

have long trusted this Jesus, but I never knew His name before." There was no change of purpose with this man, but, in the story of Jesus, the burst of light that brought unspeakable peace as he kept on in his upward tug.

Yet all this will not hold back from glad sacrifice, from free giving, from eager going to foreign mission lands a single man or woman who has been caught by Jesus' Spirit. The Master said, "Go ye." That's enough. For the largest wealth that may be given, for the keenest sacrifice that may be endured, for the strongest life that may be devoted – that is quite enough. And if more were needed – then to go, to give, to sacrifice for the sake of helping our struggling brothers yonder know Jesus, and His wondrous sacrifice and His great peace. To make them conscious of the disgustingness of sin, to bring to them a vision of Jesus' face to allure, and enchain, to give a man's will an earnest boost, when he -would choose, but cannot seem to for the suction of sin, inherited and ever growing upon his choosing powers. God sent His best. Jesus sacrificed His all in going. We'll gladly follow in such a train. Jesus is God sending His best, sacrificing His dearest, giving His most, going Himself to get men started up the hill out of the bog.

The broken tryst.

Man's break back in Eden was very hard on God. That evening early, in the twilight, God came walking in the garden to have the usual talk with His friend. He came to keep tryst. It was the usual trysting place and trysting hour, and God had the trysting spirit. We may think He came early for this bit of fellowship. He was prompt. Nothing would be allowed to disturb this appointment. But God was disappointed. It was His first disappointment. The first one to be disappointed on this earth was God. Adam had always met Him before. We may easily think met Him eagerly, jubilantly, with glad, free, open face and clinging hands.

But the man was not there this time. He failed God. He broke tryst. He stayed away. Indeed, he had gone away. God didn't fail. He was there. The man failed. They had a long distance talk. God called Adam. He was not content to come to the trysting place. He must find the missing tryster. Some folk would make God a sort of hard and dry keeper of His word: A sort of trim syllogism, dry as punk. Some seem to think Him to be as they seem to be. How our poor God has been slandered by His supposed defenders! God was not satisfied to keep the appointment. He wanted the man. He hungered for His friend, upon whom He had imprinted His own image. His heart was hungry for fellowship. He wanted the comfort of a bit of talk. So He starts at once eagerly, insistently to find the man.

That voice of God spoke out, tender, gentle, plaintive, pleading. You can just hear the soft, very soft woodsman's cry, "Hello-alo, hello, Adam, A-a-dam – here I am – waiting for you – I've kept my tryst – where are you? hello-o – hello – where – are – you?" The voice that spoke worlds into being, that brought life and beauty to all creation, that brought instant reverence and adoration from myriads of the upper world, that voice now speaks to one, two: two who were one. All the heart of God, all the power of God, in the soft voice talking to one man. God has always been after the one man, and still is.

And the breezes hushed to hear that voice with its new pleading tone. The birds stilled their song for this new music in minor mellowing tone. Silence for a moment, the breezes hushed, the birds stilled, the creation nearby held its breath, God held His heart still, that He might catch the first response to its cry. The twilight of that day had a pathetic sight. It saw a broken tryst; a lonely God; words of fellowship unspoken. A man and woman hiding. Skulking behind trees. Trees served a new purpose that evening, not a good purpose. They never were meant to hide behind. Sin perverts the use of all things.

All these weary years God has been standing wherever men are: standing, waiting, calling man back to his tryst. Among the trees, in the crowded city of man's making, He is ever calling, and eagerly, wondrously, helping everyone who answers. He is so near that a reaching hand always touches Him. The voice of the heart never misses His ear. But His love and grief shine out most on that bit of a hill, outside a city wall, on the east coast of the middle-of-the-earth sea. That is earth's tallest hill. It can be seen farthest away of any. Jesus up on that hill is God calling man back to his broken tryst.

God's wooing.

God seems to have fairly outdone Himself to get man to turn toward the old trysting place. For when a man will turn around enough to get even a glimpse of that God-Face, and a whisper of that God-Voice, he can withstand no longer.

God has taxed all the ingenuity of His love to let man know about Himself. He revealed Himself directly to the whole race at the start. He has in every generation, and in every clime, on every hilltop and valley, in every village and crowded city, been revealing Himself to the heart of every man. There cannot be found one anywhere who has not heard the quiet inner voice drawing up, and away from wrong.

In this world of wondrous beauty God is speaking. The glory-telling heavens, the winsome colouring of trees and all growing things, the soft round hills, the sublime mountains, the sea with its ever-changing mood but never-changing beneficence upon the life of the whole earth, the great blue and grey above, the soothing green below, the brighter colours in their artistic proportion, the wondrous blending – surely every bush and other green thing, every bright twinkle in the blue, everything is aflame with the presence that burns but in great love consumes not. His eyes are indeed badly bothered that cannot see; his ears in queer fix that do not hear. Yet sometimes the empty shoes seem few enough. But they are ever increasing, and will yet more and more, by retail method, with wholesale result.

But God comes closer yet in His wooing. The web of life's daily run, with its strange mixing and blending, shadings and tints, is of His weaving. He sits at life's loom ever watching and weaving. Were He but recognized oftener and His hand allowed to guide the skein, how different the weaving!

"Children of yesterday,
Heirs of to-morrow,
What are you weaving –
Labour and sorrow?
Look to your looms again;
Faster and faster
Fly the great shuttles
Prepared by the Master.
Life's in the loom,
Room for it – room!

"Children of yesterday,
Heirs of to-morrow,
Lighten the labour
And sweeten the sorrow:
Now – while the shuttles fly
Faster and faster,
Up and be at it –

At work with the Master.
He stands at your loom,
Room for Him – room!

"Children of yesterday,
Heirs of to-morrow,
Look at your fabric
Of labour and sorrow.
Seamy and dark
With despair and disaster,
Turn it – and lo,
The design of the Master.
The Lord's at the loom,
Room for Him – room."[4]

When men's eyes seemed unable to see clearly these revelations of Himself, God picked out a small tribe, and through long, patient, painstaking discipline, gave to it, for the whole world, a special revelation of Himself. In it, in the Book which preserves its records, in the Man who came through it, God came nearer yet.

In Jesus, God told out His greatness most, and His love most tenderly. Man is the fairest flower of earth's creation. It was love's fine touch that to him God should reveal Himself best and most in the fairest flower of the eternal creation. Only man could fully appreciate Jesus, God's Man, and man's Brother.

But Jesus was known only to one generation – His own generation – to one narrow strip of country, one peculiarly exclusive tribe, the very small majority of all to whom He had come. So there came to be a Book that all after-generations might know Him too. We of later generations know of Jesus through the Book, in some shape or other, before we can come to know Himself direct. And so we prize the Book above all others. Not for the Book's sake, at all, of course, but because through it we come to know Jesus. With loving reverence, we handle it, for it tells of Him, our God-brother.

Some learned folk have been much taken up with the make-up of the Book, its paper and type, and punctuation, and binding. And they

---

[4] Mary A. Lathbury

have done good service in clearing away a lot of dust and cobwebs that had been gathering on it for a long time. But we plain folk, absorbed in getting things done, do not need to wait on their conclusions. If in those pages we have found Jesus, and God in Jesus, the Book has fulfilled its mission to us.

To all directly, in nature's voice, and in our common daily life; to a nation chosen for the special purpose, and through that nation and its books; through Jesus to those who knew Him, and, by a Book telling of Him, to all following, God came, comes in His wooing, and looked, looks tenderly into man's face. Each of these paths leads straight to God, and each comes to include the others.

But chiefly in Jesus God came. Jesus is God going out in the cold black night, over the mountains, down the ravines and gullies, eagerly hunting for His lost man, getting hands, and face, and more, torn on the brambly thorn bushes, and losing His life, in the darkness, on a tree thrust in His path, but saving the man.

The Plan for Jesus' Coming

The image of God.

Man is God's darling – the king and crown of creation. The whole creation was made for him to develop and rule over and enjoy. He is in a class by himself. When he made his bad break there was just one thing left to do. God must get a new leader for His man to lead him back into all the original plan for himself. Of the whole earth man stood next to God Himself. God could not find that leader lower down. So He went higher. Jesus is God giving the race a new Leader who would withstand the lure of temptation and realize the ambition of God's heart for His darling.

The man was made in the image of God, for self-mastery, and through self-mastery for dominion over all of God's creation. That was the plan for the man. That, too, is the plan for the new Man. There is only one place to go to find God's plan for the coming One. That is in the Hebrew half of the Bible. One can hardly believe, unless he has been through the thing, how hard it is to get out of the Old Testament its vision of the coming One without any colouring from the New getting into his eyes.

We have been reading the Old Testament through the events of the New for so long that it gives a severe mental wrench to try to do anything else. Yet only so, be it sharply marked, can the plan for the coming of Jesus be gotten, and, further, only so can Jesus be understood. One must attempt to do just that to understand at all fairly what a reverent Hebrew in prophetic times expected; what such earnest Hebrews as Simeon and Anna were looking for.

I have tried to make a faithful effort to shut severely out of view the familiar facts of the gospel story for my own sake, to try to understand God's plan as it stood before there was a gospel story.

This old Hebrew picture is so full of details that are found in the reality that one who has not actually gone studiously over the Old separately will be very likely to think that the New Testament details are being read into the Old. If that be so, it is urgently requested that such an opinion be held off until the old Hebrew pages have been carefully examined as outlined in the study notes, that you may get the refreshment of a great surprise.

It must be kept keenly in mind that there is a difference between God's plan and that which He knows ahead will occur. Sovereignty does not mean that everything God plans comes to pass. Nor that everything that comes to pass is God's plan. Clearly it has not been so. It does mean that through very much that is utterly contrary to His Plan He works out, in the long run, His great purpose. He works His own purpose out of a tough tangled network of contrary purposes; but in doing it never infringes upon man's liberty of action. He yields and bends, and, with a patience beyond our comprehension, waits, that in the end He may win through our consent. And so not only is His purpose saved, but man is saved and character is made in the process.

The plan is a detail of the purpose. There is one unfailing purpose through continual breakings of the plan. God's purpose remains unchanging through all changes. Yet here not only is His purpose unbroken, but His plan is to work out in the end unbroken too, though suffering a very serious break midway.

The plan goes back to the first broken plan. There was dominion or kingship of the earth by a masterful man bearing the image and imprint of God. All this was lost. Through loss of contact with God came the blurring of the image and the loss of self-mastery. Through loss of these came loss of dominion. These are to be restored – all three. This is the key to the plan for the coming of Jesus. A universal dominion, under the lead of a Master-Man, in God's image, and through these a restoration of blessing to all the earth of men. This is the one continuous theme of the old Hebrew writings. The emphasis swings now to one aspect, now to another, but through all the one thought is a king, a world-wide kingdom bringing blessing to all creation.

But if Jesus was to lead man back He must first get alongside, close up, on the same level. This was the toughest part of the whole thing. The hardest part in saving a man is getting the man's consent to be saved. There is no task tougher than trying to help a man who thinks he doesn't need help, even though his need may be extreme. You may throw a blanket over a horse's head and get it out of a burning stable or barn; or a lasso over a bull's head to get it where you want, but man cannot be handled that way. He must be led. The tether that draws must be fastened inside, his will. He must be lifted from inside. That is a bit of the God-image in him. And so God's most difficult task was getting inside the man that had shut Him out.

Fastening a tether inside.

And a long time it took. That it took so long, measured by the calendar, suggests how great was the resistance to be overcome. A long round-about road it does seem that God took. Yet it was the shortest. The circle route is always the shortest. It is nature's way. Nature always follows the line of least resistance. The eagle, descending, comes in circles, the line of least resistance. Water running out of a bowl through the hole in the bottom follows the circuitous route – the easiest.

God's longest way around was the shortest way into man's heart. Standards had to be changed. New standards made. Yet in making a standard there must be a starting point. God's bother was to get a starting point. When man was too impure in his ingrained ideas to receive any idea of what purity meant, things were in bad shape. When he was grubbing content in the gutter, how was he ever to be gotten up to the highlands, when you couldn't even lift his eyes over the curb stone? All the prohibitions of the Mosaic code are but faithful mirrors of man's condition. A wholly new standard had to be set up. That was God's task. It must be set up through men if they were to be attracted to it. So God started on His longest-way-around-shortest road into man's heart.

A man is chosen. Through this man, by the slow processes of generations, a nation is grown. Yet a nation only in numbers at first; in no other sense; a mob of men. Then this mob is worked upon. They are led through experiences that will make them soft to new impressions. Then slowly, laboriously, by child-training methods, the new standard is brought to them. Yet after centuries the best attained is only that their tenacious fingers have hold of a form, not yet the spirit. Yet this is an immense gain.

By and by this is the pedigree: A man, a family, tribes, a nation, a strong nation, a broken nation, a literature, ragged remnants of a nation, an ideal the like of which could not be found anywhere on earth, and a book embodying that ideal written as with acid-point in metal, as with sharpest chisel in hardest stone.

At last a start was made. God had gotten a hook inside man's will to which He could tie His tether, and draw, lovingly, tenderly, tenaciously, persistently, draw up out of the mire, toward the highlands, toward Himself.

The first touches on the canvas.

This old Hebrew picture is found to be a mosaic made up of bits gathered here and there, scattered throughout the Book. Some of the bits are of very quiet sober colours found in obscure corners. Others are bright. When brought together all blend into one with wondrous, fine beauty. The first bit is of grave hue. It comes at the very beginning. There is to be sharp enmity, then a crisis, resulting in a fatal wound for the head of evil, with scars for the victor.

After this earliest general statement there are three distinct groups or periods of prediction regarding the coming One. During the making of the nation, during its high tide of strength and glory under David and his son, during the time of its going to pieces. As the national glory is departing, the vision takes on its most glorious colouring. The first of these is during the making of the nation. As the man who is to be father of the chosen family is called away from his kinfolk to a preparatory isolation, he is cheered with the promise that his relationship is to be a relationship of leadership and of great blessing to the whole earth. This is repeated to his son and to his grandson, as each in turn becomes head of the family. As his grandson, the father of the twelve men whose names become the tribe names, is passing away he prophetically sees the coming leadership narrowed to Judah, through whom the great Leader is to come.

Later yet, in a story of divination and superstition characteristic of the time, a strange prophet is hired by an enemy to pronounce a curse upon the new nation. This diviner is taken possession of by the Spirit of God, and forced to utter what is clearly against his own mercenary desires. He sees a coming One, in the future, who is to smite Israel's enemies and rule victoriously.

During the last days of Moses that man, great to the whole race, speaks a word that sinks in deep. In his good-bye message he says there is some One coming after him, who will be to them as he had been, one of their own kin, a deliverer, king, lawgiver, a wise, patient, tender judge and teacher. The nation never forgot that word. When John the Baptist came, they asked, "Art thou the prophet?"

The second group of predictions is found during the nation's strength and glory. To David comes the promise that the royal house he has founded is to be forever, in contrast with Saul's, even though his successors may fail to keep faith with God. It is most striking to note how much this meant to David. He accepts it as meaning that the nation's Messiah and the world's King is to be of his own blood. "Thou hast spoken also of thy servant's house for a great while to come." Then follows this very significant sentence: "And this is (or, must be) the law of the man (or, the Adam)." This promise must refer to the plan of God concerning the woman's seed, the man, the Adam.

At the close, when the tether of life is slipping its hold, this vision of the coming greater Heir promised by God evidently fills his eye. He says:

"There shall lie One that ruleth over men;
A righteous One, that ruleth in the fear of God.
And it shall be then as the light of the morning,
When the sun ariseth, A morning without clouds,
The tender grass springing out of the earth through
clear shining after rain."
"Verily, my own house has not been so with God;
Yet hath He made with me an everlasting covenant,
Ordered in all things and sure.
For this covenant is now all my comfort and all my
desire,
Although he has not yet brought it to pass."[5]

---

[5] Nathaniel Parker Willis

This seems to be the setting of those psalms of his referring to the coming One. It was to be expected that his poetical fire would burn with such a promise and conception. In the Second Psalm he sees this coming Heir enthroned as God's own Son, and reigning supremely over the whole earth despite the united opposition of enemies. In the One Hundred and Tenth Psalm this Heir is sharing rule at God's right hand while waiting the subduing of all enemies. He is to be divine, a king, and more, a priest-king. Surrounded by a nation of volunteers full of youthful vigour He will gain a decisive victory over the head of the allied enemies, and yet be Himself undisturbed in the continual freshness of His vigour. And all this rests upon the unchanging oath of Jehovah.

David's immediate heir found his father's pen, and in the Seventy-second Psalm repeats, with his own variations, his father's vision of the coming greater Heir. While there is repetition of the kingdom being world-wide and unending, with all nations in subjection, the chief emphasis is put upon the blessing to that great majority – the poor. They are to be freed from all oppression, to have full justice done them, with plenty of food to eat, and increased length of life.

That David's expectation had thoroughly permeated his circle is shown in the joyous Forty-fifth Psalm, written by one of the court musicians. It addresses the coming One as more than human, having great beauty and graciousness, reigning in righteousness, victoriously, with a queen of great beauty, and a princely posterity for unending generations.

A full-length picture in colours.

These are but the beginnings. It is in the prophetic books, the third of the groups, that the full picture with its brightest colouring is found. The picture is not only winsome beyond all comparison and glorious, but stupendous in its conception and its sweep. It is most notable that, as the flood-tide of the nation's prosperity ebbs from its highest mark, the vision to the prophetic eye of a coming glory grows steadily in brightness and in distinctness. As the great kings go, the great prophets come. It is to them we must turn for the full-length picture.

The one continuous subject of the prophets is the coming King and kingdom and attendant events. Immediate historical events furnish the setting, but with a continual swinging to the coming future greatness. The yellow glory light of the coming day is never out of the prophetic sky. Its reflection is never out of the prophetic eye. Jeremiah is the one most absorbed in the boiling of the political pot of his own strenuous time, but even he at times lifts his head and gets such glimpses of the coming glory as make him mix some rose tincture with the jet black ink he uses.

The common thread running through the fabric of the prophetic books clear from Isaiah to Malachi is the phrase "in that day." Sometimes it thickens into "the day of the Lord," "the great day of the Lord," "Jehovah hath a great day," "at that time." About this thread is woven in turn the whole series of stirring scenes and events that are to mark the coming time. Sometimes it is of local application; most times of the future time, and a few times the meaning slides from one to the other, touching both.

Over all of these pages is the shadow of Somebody coming down the aisle of the ages, who is to be the world's Master. The figure of a man, large to gigantic size, majestic, yet kindly as well as kingly, looms out through these lines before the reader's face. The old idea of God Himself dwelling in the midst of the people, sharing their life, made familiar by Eden, by the flame-tipped mount and the glory-filled tent, comes out again. For this coming One is said to be God Himself. But more than that He is to be a man, and a son of man; man bred of man. The blending of the two, God and man, is pointed to in the unprecedented thing of a pure virgin birth for this one. God and a pure maiden join themselves in His coming. He is to be of native Hebrew stock, in direct descent from the great David, and born in David's native village. Of course He is to be a king as was David, but unlike that ancestor, to be not only a king, but a priest, and a preacher and teacher.

The kingdom he will set up will be like Himself in its blending of the human and divine. Its origin is not human, but divine. The capital is to be Zion or Jerusalem. It will be marked by the glorious presence of God Himself visibly present to all eyes. The characteristics of the kingdom are of peculiar attractiveness, at any time, to any people of this poor old blood-stained, gun-ploughed battle-field of an earth. The stronger traits that men commonly think of as desirable are combined with traits that have been reckoned by men of all generations as absurdly, unpractically idealistic.

There will be vengeance upon all enemies, who have been using Israel as a common football, and great victory. Yet, strangely, these will be gotten without the use of violent force, and will be followed by great peace. The kingdom is to be established in loving-kindness and marked to an unparalleled degree by a sense of right and justice to all. This feature is emphasized over and over again, with refreshing frequency to those so eager for such a revolutionary change in their affairs. Absolute gentle fairness and impartiality will decide all difficulties arising. Even the most friendless and the most obnoxious thing will be fairly judged.

That great universal majority, the poor, will be especially guarded and cared for. There will be no hungry people, nor cold, nor poorly clad; no unemployed, begging for a chance to earn a dry crust, and no workers fighting for a fair share of the fruit of their sweat-wet toil. But there are tenderer touches yet upon this canvas. Broken hearts will be healed up, prison doors unhung, broken family circles complete again. It is to be a time of great rejoicing by the common people. Yet all this will be brought about, not immediately, but gradually, following the natural law of growth; though the beginning will be marked by a great crisis, coming suddenly.

The effect upon Israel nationally is to be tremendous, sweepingly reversing the conditions under which most of these predictions are made. Israel is to become a Spirit-baptized nation, wholly swayed by the Spirit of God, and that gracious sway never to be withdrawn. All judgments for her sins are removed and all impurity thoroughly cleansed away. Possession of their own land is assured. And the capital city is to become a holy place from which, in common with the whole land, all impurity has been cleansed away. All weakness and disability are gone, and full freedom from the exactions of her former enemies to be enjoyed. Not only is Israel to be at peace with all nations, but, far more, is to have the leadership of the nations of the earth, and leadership of the highest sort – in a world-wide spiritual movement, in the day when the Spirit of God is to be poured out upon all flesh.

This leadership is to be a glorious and absolute supremacy among all the nations of the earth. And yet this is not to be by man's method of conquest, but of their own earnest accord all nations will come a-running eagerly, voluntarily, with all their wealth and resources for the building up and service of Israel. In that time the Hebrew capital Jerusalem will likewise be the capital of the earth.

No less radical and sweeping will be the changes in Israel personally, individually. The people are to be made over new within. The modern word for this sort of thing is regeneration. The old-fashioned word is a new heart – a new spirit. The change is to be at the core; a change of the sort. With this will come a marked spirit of devotion to God, and a peculiar open-mindedness to the truth. There will be an absence of all sickness and a decided increase in length of life and great increase in numbers. There will be no longer any disappointment in plans, and the sense of slavish fear, which is universal, not only with all the race, but through all time, will be utterly absent. Israel is to be a nation of persons with thrilled hearts and radiant faces.

Back to Eden.

The effect upon all the nations of the earth is a large part of the background of the picture. Through Israel's advancement under the new order, every other nation is to come back to God. The outpouring of the Spirit upon Israel is to be followed by an outpouring upon all flesh. There are the two outpourings of God's Spirit in these old prophetic pages. This will be followed by a universal, voluntary coming to Israel for religious instruction. She becomes the teacher of the nations regarding God, until by and by the whole earth shall be filled with the knowledge of the only God. Her influence upon them for good will be as the heavy fertilizing eastern dews and the life-giving showers are to vegetation.

But further yet, Israel is to be the only medium of God's blessing upon the nations – the only channel. Those refusing her leadership will, for lack of vital sap, die of dry rot. The wondrous blessing enjoyed by this central nation, the un-hinging of dungeon doors, the opening of blind eyes, the mellowing of all the hard conditions of life, the reign of simple, full justice to all, is to be shared with all the nations. Israel's peace with all nations is to become a universal peace between and among all nations.

But there's still more. There are to follow certain radical changes in the realm of nature. Splendid rivers of water are to flow through Jerusalem, necessitating changes in the formation of the land there. The fortress capital of the Jews strongly entrenched among the Judean hills is to become, as the world's metropolis, a mighty city, with rivers to float the earth's commerce. The light of the sun and moon will be greatly increased, and yet this greatly intensified light will become at Jerusalem a shadow cast by the greater light of the presence of God. A devout Hebrew would associate this back with the light of the Presence-cloud in the Arabian barrens. While the devout Christian will likely, quickly think forward from that to the light that was one time as the sun, and, again, above the sun's brightness. Naturally, with this comes a renewed fertility of the earth's soil, and the removal of the curse upon vegetation. Before the healing light and heat, the poisonous growth, the blight of drought and of un-tempered heat disappear. There is to be a new earth and above it a new heaven.

To complete the picture, the animal creation is to undergo changes as radical as these. Beasts dangerous because of ferocity and because of treachery and poisonous qualities will be wholly changed. Meat-eating beasts will change their habit of diet, and eat grain and herbs. There will be a mutual cessation of cruelty to animals by man and of danger to man from animals, for all violence will have ceased.

And then the climax is capped by repeated assurances that this marvellous kingdom will be as extensive as the earth and absolutely unending.

The whole thing, be it keenly noticed, is simply a return to the original condition. In the Eden garden was the presence of God, a masterful man in the likeness of God, with full dominion over all creation. There was full accord in all nature, and perfect fellowship between man and nature.

All this is to come to pass through the coming One. He is the key that unlocks this wondrous future. Through all, above all, growing ever bigger, is the shadowy majestic figure of a Man coming. His personal characteristics make Him very attractive and winsome. He will be of unusual mental keenness both in understanding and in wisdom, combined with courage of a high order, and, above all, dominated by a deep reverential, a keenly alert, love for God. He will be beautiful in person and, in sharp contrast with earth's kings, while marked personally with that fine dignity and majesty unconscious of itself, will be gentle and unpretentious in His bearing. His relations with God are direct and very intimate, being personally trained and taught by Him. Backed by all of His omnipotence, He will be charged with the carrying out of His great plans for the chosen people and through them for the world.

In a fine touch it is specially said that "He will judge the poor." Poor folk, who haven't money to employ lawyers to guard their interests, and haven't time for much education to know better how to protect themselves against those who would take advantage of them – the poor, that's the overwhelming majority of the whole world – He will be their judge. They will have a friend on the bench. But He will have this enormous advantage in judging all men, poor and otherwise, that He will not need to decide by what folk tell Him, nor by outside things. He will be able to read down into the motives and back into the life.

Such is the plan for the coming One outlined in these old pages. To many a modern all this must seem like the wildest dream of an utterly unpractical enthusiast. Yet, mark it keenly, this is the conception of this old Hebrew book that has been, and is, the world's standard of morals and of wisdom. The book revered above all others by the most thoughtful men, of all shades of belief. It is striking how the parts of this stupendous conception fit and hold together. There is a mature symmetry about the whole scheme. For instance, the changes in the light of sun and moon run parallel with the changes in growth and in the healthfulness and longer lives of man. Increased light removes both disease and its cause, and gives new life and lengthened life.

Surely these Hebrews are a great people in their visions. And a vision is an essential of greatness. Yet this sublime conception of their future is not regarded as a visionary dream, but calmly declared to be the revealed plan of God for them, and through them for the earth. And that, too, not by any one man, but successively through many generations of men. The prophetic spirit of the nation in the midst of terrible disaster and of moral degradation never loses faith in its ultimate greatness, through the fulfilling of its mission to the nations of the earth.

Is it to be wondered at that the devout Israelite, who believed in his book and its vision, pitched his tent on the hilltop, with his eye ever scanning the eastern horizon, for the figure of the coming One? And when eyes grown dim for the long looking believed that at last that figure was seen, the heart breathed out its grateful relief in "Now lettest thou thy servant depart in peace, for my eyes have seen."

Strange dark shadowing's.

But, too, there is in this vision of glory something very different, so mixed in that it won't come out. There are dark shadows from the first touch upon the canvas. Always there is a bitter, malignant enemy. There is decisive victory, but it comes only after sharp, hard, long-continued fighting. But in the latter parts, that is, in David's time, and intensifying in the later pages, there is something darker yet. Through these lines run forebodings, strange, weird, sad forebodings of evil. There are dark grey threads, inky black threads, that do not harmonize with the pattern being woven. And the weavers notice it, and wonder, and yet are under a strange impulse to weave on without understanding.

Their coming One is to be a king, but there is the distinct consciousness that there would be for Him terrible experiences through which He must pass, and to which He would yield on His way to the throne. The very conception seems to involve a contradiction which puzzles these men who write them down. Like a lower minor strain running through some great piece of music are the few indications of what God foreknew, though He did not foreplan, would happen to Jesus. A sharp line must always be drawn between what God plans and what He knows will happen. The soft sobbing of what God could see ahead runs as a minor sad cadence through the story of His plans.

Sometimes these forebodings are acted out. In the light of the Gospels we can easily see very striking likenesses between the experiences in which keen suffering precedes great victory, of such national leaders as Joseph and David, and the experiences of Jesus. Here is God's plan of atonement by blood, involving suffering, but with no such accompaniments of hatred and cruelty as Jesus went through. Read backward, Jesus' experience on the cross is seen to bear striking resemblances, in part, to this old scheme of atonement; yet only in part: the parts concerning His character and the results; but not the manner of his death, nor the spirit of the actors.

Then there are the few direct specific passages predicting a stormy trip for the king before the haven is reached. There is a vividness of detail in the very language here, that catches us, familiar with after events, as it could not those who first heard. There is the Twenty-second Psalm, with its broken sentences, as though blurted out between heart-breaking sobs; and then the wondrous change, in the latter part, to victory through this terrible experience. And the scanty but vivid lines in the Sixty-ninth Psalm. There is that great throbbing fifty-third of Isaiah, with its beginning back in the close of the fifty-second, and the striking ahead of its key-note in the fiftieth chapter.

Daniel listens with awe deepening ever more as Gabriel tells him that the coming Prince is to be "cut off." To the returned exiles rebuilding the temple Zechariah acts out a parable in which Jehovah is priced at thirty pieces of silver, the cost of a common slave. And a bit later God speaks of a time when "they shall look upon Me (or Him) whom they have pierced." And later yet, a still more significant phrase is used, as identifying the divine character of the sufferer, where God speaks of a sword being used "against the man that is My Fellow," adding, "Strike the shepherd, and the sheep shall be scattered." It is God's Fellow – one on a par with Himself – against whom the opposition is directed.

Such is the great vision in these Hebrew pages of the plan for the coming One. There is a throne on a high mountain peak bathed in wondrous sublime glory, but the writers are puzzled at a dark valley of the shadow of death through which the king seems to be obliged to pick His way up to the throne.

Jesus is to be God's new Man leading man back on the road into the divine image again, with full mastery of his masterly powers, and through mastery into full dominion again; but the road back seems to be contested, and the new Man gets badly scarred as He fights through and up to victory.

The Tragic Break in The Plan

The Jerusalem climate.

Then Jesus came. His coming was greeted with great gladness above, and great silence below. Above, the stars sent a special messenger to bid Him welcome to the earth they lightened and brightened. Below, the rusty hinges of earth's inn refused to swing for Him. So man failing, the lower creation shared room with Him.

Above, was the sweetest music, the music of heaven. Three times the music of heaven is mentioned: at the creation, at this coming of Jesus, at the coming crowning of Jesus in John's Revelation. Below, the only music was that of the babe's holy young mother, God's chosen one to mother His Son, crooning to her babe; and the gentle lowing in minor key of the oxen whose stall He shared. Above, the great glory shining, the messenger of God speaking a message of peace and love. Below, only darkness and silence.

Among the cultured leaders of the city of David, and of Solomon, and of God's once glorified temple, there were no ears for the message, nor eyes for the glory. They had gone deaf and blind Godward long before. To them came no message, for no door was open. To simple men of nature who lived with the stars and the hills and the sheep, came the new shining of the glory, and the wondrous messenger and message. Their doors were open. They practised looking up. Of course neither city nor country mattered, nor matters. God always speaks into the upturned ear and looks into the upturned face.

And so Jesus came. With all of its contrasts it was a winsome[6] coming. A pure young mother nursing her babe; the babe with its sweet wondrous face, a fresh act of God indeed; the simple unselfish cattle; the bright stars; the Glory shining; the sudden flood of music; the Lord's messenger; the message – a very winsome coming.

---

[6] attractive or appealing in appearance or character

He came into the peculiar climate of Jerusalem. Jerusalem is Judea. Out of the Babylonian remnant of Israel had come great men, true leaders, with great zeal for the city, and the temple, and the temple service, and for the law. They made the mould in which this later Jerusalem was cast. But that mould retaining its old form, had now become filled with the baser metals. The high ideals of the new makers of the city had shrunk into mere ideas. The small, strongly entrenched ruling circle were tenacious sticklers for traditions as interpreted by themselves. That fine old word conservative (with an underneath meaning of "what we prefer") was one of their sweetest morsels. Underneath their great pride as Moses' successors, the favoured custodians of the nation's most sacred treasures, was a passionate love for gold. The temple service was secretly organized on the profit-sharing plan, with the larger share, as usual, for the organizers.

That hardest thing in the whole range of human action to overcome, either by God or man or the devil – prejudice – they had, in the Simon-pure form, superlatively refined. The original treasure of God's Word was about as much overlaid and hidden away by writings about it as – it has been in some other times. Of course they were looking for a Messiah, the one hope of their sacredly guarded literature. But He must be the sort that they wanted, and – could use.

Herod the King was a man of great ability, great ambition, great passion, and great absence of anything akin to conscience. But the virtual ruler was the high priest. His office was bargained for, bought and sold for the money and power it controlled in the way all too familiar to corrupt political life in all times, and not wholly unknown in our own. The old spiritual ideals of Moses, and Samuel, preached amid degeneracy by Elijah and Isaiah, were buried away clear out of sight by mere formalism, though still burning warm and tender in the hearts of a few. This was the atmosphere of the old national capital into which Jesus came.

The Bethlehem fog.

Then it was that Jesus came. Strange to say, there is a shadow over His coming from the beginning. A grey chilling shadow of the sort of grey that a stormy sky sometimes shows, grey tingeing into slate black. Yet it was the coming that made the shadow. It takes light, and some thick thing like a block, and some distance for perspective, to make a shadow. The nearer the light to the block thing the blacker the shadow. Here the light came close to some thick blocks; of stupid thickness;

human blocks grown more toughly thick by the persistent resisting of any such transparent thing as light.

This was a foggy shadow. A fog is always made by influences from below. A lowering temperature chills the air, and brings down its moisture in the shape of a grey subtle pervasive mist, that blurs the outlook, and often gathers and holds black smoke, and mean poisonous odours and gases from bog and swamp. Such a fog endangers both health and life. This was just such a shadowing fog. There was a decided drop in the temperature, a sudden chill, a fog formed that sucked up the poison of the marshes, and threatened to stifle the baby breath of the new-born King.

A subtle, intangible, but terribly sure something haunts and hunts the King from the first. His virgin mother is suspected by the one nearest her of the most serious offense that can be charged against a woman. The shadow that later grew to inky blackness came ahead of the man, and, under the stable eaves, waited grimly His arrival. The feverish green of Herod's eyes will be content with nothing but a new, bright, running red, and plenty of it. Satan's plan of killing was started early. He was not particular about the way it was done. The first attempt was at Bethlehem. The venomous spittle oozed out there first. But he must move along natural channels: just now, a murderous king's jealous dread of a possible rival.

The first hint of the actual coming of the long expected One is from the star-students of the east. Their long journey and eager questioning bring the birth of Jesus before the official circle of the nation. It is most significant that His birth causes at once a special meeting of the nation's ruling body. Herod was troubled, of course. But – all Jerusalem was troubled with him. Here is a surprising sympathy. It reflects at once vividly the situation. It was strangely suggestive that news of their King coning should trouble these national leaders. These devout star-watchers are wise in the source of information they came to. These leaders knew. They quickly pointed out the spot where the coming One should be born.

A pure virgin under cruel suspicion, a roomless inn, a village filled with heart-broken mothers, a quick flight on a dark night to a foreign land by a young mother and her babe, the stealthy retirement into a secluded spot away from his native province, a fellow feeling between a red-handod king and tho nation's leaders – ugh! an ugly, deadly fog.

The man sent ahead.

A high fence of silence shuts out from view the after years. Just one chink of a crack appears in the fence, peering through which, one gets a suggestion of beautiful simplicity, of the true, natural human growing going on beyond the fence.

When mature years are reached, the royal procession is formed. A man is sent ahead to tell of the King's coming. John was Jesus' diplomatic representative, His plenipotentiary extraordinary; that is, the one man specifically sent to represent Him to the nation whose King He was. Treatment of John was treatment of Jesus. A slight done him was slighting his sovereign Master. If Sir Henry Mortimer Durand[7] were to be slighted or treated discourteously by the American authorities, it would be felt at London as a slight upon the King[8], the government, and the nation they represent. Any indignity permitted to be done on American soil to von Stuckenburg[9] would be instantly resented by Kaiser William as personal to himself. John was Jesus' Durand, His von Stuckenburg, His Whitelaw Reid[10]. And no diplomat ever used more tactful language than this John when questioned about his Master. In Jesus' own simile, John was His best man. Jesus was a bridegroom. John stood by His side as His most intimate friend.

Jesus and John are constantly interwoven in the events of Jesus' career. We moderns, who do everything by the calendar, have been puzzled in the attempt to piece together these events into an exact calendar arrangement. And the beautiful mosaic of the Gospels has been cut up to make a new, modern, calendar mosaic. But these writers see things by events, not by dates. They have in mind four great events, and about these their story clusters. And in these Jesus and John are inextricably interwoven. First is John's wilderness ministry, heading up in his presenting Jesus to the nation. Then John's violent seizure, and Jesus' withdrawal from the danger zone. Then John's death, and Jesus' increased caution in His movements. Then Jesus' death. John comes, points to Jesus, and goes. Jesus comes, walks a bit with John, reaches beyond him and then goes, too.

John baptized. That is, he used a purifying rite in connection with his preaching. It helps to remember the distinction between baptism as

---

[7] English Ambassador to America
[8] King George III
[9] Imperial German Ambassador to America
[10] US Ambassador to the United Kingdom 1905 - 1912

practised in the Christian Church, and as practised by John, and by Jesus in His early ministry. In the church, baptism has come to be regarded as a dedicatory rite by some, and by others an initial and confessional rite. But in the first use of it, by John and Jesus, it was a purifying rite. It was a confession too, but of sin, and the need of cleansing, not, as later, of faith in a person, or a creed, although it did imply acceptance of a man's leadership. To a Hebrew mind it was preaching by symbol as well as by word. The official deputation sent from Jerusalem to look John up asked why he should be using a purifying rite if he were neither the Christ, nor Elijah, nor the prophet. They could understand the appropriateness of either of these three persons using such a rite in connection with his preaching as indicating the national need of cleansing. And in the beginning Jesus for a time, through His disciples, joined in John's plan of baptizing those who confessed sorrow for sin.

Jesus acknowledged John as His own representative, and honoured him as such, from first to last. He gives him the strongest approval and backing. The national treatment of John always affects Jesus' movements. When, toward the close, His authority is challenged, He at once calls attention to the evident authority of His forerunner and refuses to go farther.

A trace of that ominous, puzzling foreboding noticed in the Old Testament vision of the coming One creeps in here. Pointing to Jesus, John says, "Behold the lamb of God, who beareth (away) the sin of the world." Why did John say that? We read his words backward in the light of Calvary. But he could not do that, and did not. He knew only a King coming. Why? Even as Isaiah fifty-third, and Psalm twenty-second were written, the writers there, the speaker here, impelled to an utterance, the meaning of which, was not clear to themselves.

This relation and intimacy between these two, John and Jesus, must be steadily kept in mind.

The contemptuous rejection.

From the very first, though Jesus was accepted by individuals of every class, He was rejected by the nation. This is the twin-fact standing out in boldest outline through the Gospel stories. The nation's rejection began with the formal presentation of Him to it by John. First was the simple refusal to accept, then the decision to reject, then the determination that everybody else should reject too. First, that He should not be admitted to their circle, then that He should be kept out of their circle, and then that He should be kept out of every circle. There are these three distinct stages in the rejection from the Jordan waters to the Calvary Hill.

First came the contemptuous rejection. John was a great man. Made of the same rugged stuff as the old prophets, he was more than they in being the King's own messenger and herald. In his character he was great as the greatest, though not as great in privilege as those living in the kingdom. He preached and baptized. With glowing eyes of fire, deep-set under shaggy brows, and plain vigorous speech which, if pricked, would ooze out red life, he told of the sin that must be cleaned out as a preparation for the coming One. And to all who would, he applied the cleansing rite.

He had great drawing power. Away from cultured Jerusalem on the hilltops down to the river bottoms, and the stony barrens of the Jordan; from the Judean hill country, away from the stately temple service with its music and impressive ritual, to his simple open-air, plain, fervid preaching, he drew men. All sorts came, the proud Pharisee, the cynical Sadducee, the soldiers, the publicans, farmers, shepherds, tradespeople – all came. His daily gatherings represented the whole people. The nation came to his call. It was the unconscious testimony of the nation to his rugged greatness and to his divine mission. They were impelled to come, and listen, and do, and questioningly wonder if this can be the promised national leader.

One day a committee came from the Jewish Senate to make official inquiry as to who he claimed to be. With critical, captious questions they demand his authority. True to his mission and his Master, he said, "I am not the One, but sent to tell you that He's coming, and so near that it's time to get ready." Then the next day, as Jesus walks quietly through the crowd, probably just back from the wilderness, he finishes his reply to the deputation. With glowing eyes intently riveted upon Jesus, and finger pointing, before the alert eyes of his hundreds of hearers – Pharisees, Sadducees, official committee, Roman soldiers, and common folk – he said in clear, ringing tones, "That is He: the coming One!"

No more dramatic, impressive presentation could have been made of Jesus to the nation. To their Oriental minds it would be peculiarly significant, Mark keenly the result. On the part of the leaders utter silence There could be no more cutting expression of their contempt. With eyebrows uplifted, eyes coldly questioning, their lips slightly curling, or held close together and pursed out, and shoulders shrugging, their contempt, utter disgusted contempt, could not be more loudly expressed. If they had had the least disposition to believe John's words about Jesus, even so far as to investigate patiently and thoroughly, how different would their conduct have been! But – only silence. And silence long continued. Jesus gave them plenty of time before the next step was taken. No silence ever spoke in louder voice. That same day five thoughtful men of that same throng did investigate, and were satisfied, and gave at once loyal, loving allegiance.

A few months later, the Passover Feast drew crowds from everywhere to Jerusalem. Jesus coming into the temple areas, with the crowds, one day, is struck at once with the strange scene. Instead of reverent, holy quiet, as worshippers approached the dwelling-place of God, with their offerings of penitence and worship, the busy bustle of a market-place greets His ears. The noise of cattle and sheep being driven here and there, the pavement like an unkempt barnyard, loud, discordant voices of men handling the beasts and bargaining over exchange rates at the brokers' tables – strange scene. Is it surprising that His ear and eye and heart, perhaps fresh from a bit of quiet morning talk with His Father, were shocked? Here, where everything should have called to devotion, everything jarred.

Quietly and quickly putting some bits of knotted string together, He started the stock out, doubtless against the protests of the keepers. With flashing light out of those keen eyes, He tipped over the tables, spilling out their precious greedy coins, and ordered the crates of pigeons removed. But all with no suggestion of any violence used toward anybody. Reluctantly, perhaps angrily, wholly against their plans and wishes, the crowd, impelled by something in this unknown Man, with no outer evidence of authority, goes. It is a remarkable tribute, both to the power of His personal presence and to His executive faculty.

Of course the thing made trouble. It was the talk of the town, and of all the foreigners for days after. The leaders were aroused and angered, deeply angered. This stranger had kicked up a pretty muss with His inconvenient earnestness and inconsiderate quoting of Scripture. It was a practical assumption of superior authority over them. It was an assumption of the truth of John's ignored claim that He was the promised King.

Was not this arrangement in the temple area a great convenience for the many strangers, who were their brothers and guests; a real kindly act of hospitality? Yes – and was it not, too, a finely organized bit of business for profiting by these strangers, a using of their proper authority over the temple territory to transfer their brothers' foreign coins safely over to their own purses? Aye, it was a transmuting of their holy offices into gold by the alchemy of their coarse, greedy touch.

Jesus' conduct was the keenest sort of criticism of these rulers, before the eyes of the nation and of the thousands of pilgrims present. These leaders never forgave this humiliating rebuke of themselves. It made their nerves raw to His touch ever after. Here is the real reason of all their after bitter dislike. They had a sensitive pocket-nerve. It was a sort of pneumogastric[11] nerve so close did it come to their lives. Jesus touched it roughly. It never quit aching. Scratch all their later charges against Him and under all is this sore spot. The tree of the cross began growing its wood that day. Their hot, captious demand for authority, meant as much for the ears of the crowd as for His, brought from Jesus, who read His future in their hearts, a reply which they could not understand. They asked their question for the crowd to hear, He replied for His disciples to remember in the after years. There could be no evidence of authority more significant than this temple incident.

His first public work was done at this time. The great throng of pilgrims from around the world, attracted to Him by this simple daring act of leadership, witnessed a group of mighty acts during these Passover days. The angry leaders had critically asked for "signs" of His authority. He gave them in abundance, not in response to their captious demand, but doubtless, as always, in response to pressing human needs. The result was that many persons accepted Him, but the nation in its rulers, maintained their attitude of angered, contemptuous silence. But underneath that surface the pot is beginning to boil.

Of all the members of the national Senate, one, just one, comes to make personal inquiry, and sift this man's claim sincerely and candidly. And he, be it marked, chooses a darkened hour for that visit. That night hour speaks volumes of the smouldering passion under their contempt. That Jesus recognized fully their attitude and just what it meant comes out in that quiet evening talk. To that sincere inquirer, He frankly Jays, "You people won't receive the witness that John and I have brought you." He was pleading before a court that stubbornly refuses testimony of fact. And to this honest seeker, whom we must all love for his sincerity, He reveals His inner consciousness of a tragic break coming,

---

[11] Gordon seems to be referring to Cranial Nerves – though the understanding of this at the time was limited. He seems to be intimating that the "pocket-nerve" was like a tooth-ache!

with a pleading word for personal trust, and a saddened "men love darkness."

With the going away of the Passover crowds, Jesus leaves the national capital, and assists in the sort of work John was doing. His power to draw men, and men's eagerness for Him, stand out sharply at once. John had drawn great crowds of all classes. Jesus drew greater crowds. Multitudes eagerly accepted John's teaching and accepted baptism from him. As it turned out, greater multitudes of people, under the very eyes of these ignoring, contemptuous leaders, accepted Jesus' leadership. John baptized. Jesus baptized through His disciples. These leaders in their questioning of John had tacitly acknowledged the propriety of "the Christ" using such a rite. Jesus follows the line of least resistance, and fitted into the one phase of His work which they had recognized as proper.

The pitiable fact stands out that the only result with them is a wordy strife about the relative success of these two, Jesus and John. The most that their minds, steeped in jealousies and rivalries, ever watching with badger eyes to undercut someone else, could see, was a rivalry between these two men. John's instant open-hearted disclaimer made no impression upon them. They seemed not impressionable to such disinterested loyalty.

A little later, probably not much, John's ruggedly honest preaching against sin came too close home to suit Herod. He promptly shuts up the preacher in prison, with no protest from the nation's leaders. These leaders had developed peculiar power in influencing their civil rulers by the strenuousness of their protests. That they permitted the imprisonment of John with no word of protest, was a tacit throwing overboard of John's own claims, of John's claims for Jesus, and of Jesus' own claim.

Here is the first sharp crisis. From the first, the circle of national leaders characterized by John, the writer of the Gospel, as "the Jews," including the inner clique of chief priests and the Pharisees, ignored Jesus; with silent contempt, coldly, severely ignored. This was before the temple-cleansing affair. That intensified their attitude toward the next stage. They had to proceed cautiously, because the crowd was with Jesus. And full well these keen leaders knew the ticklishness of handling a fanatical Oriental mob, as subsequent events showed. Now John is imprisoned, with the consent of these leaders, possibly through their connivance.

Jesus keenly and quickly grasps the situation. First ignored, then made the subject of evil gossip, the temple clash, and now His closest friend subjected to violence, His own rejection is painfully evident. He makes a number of radical changes. His place of activity is changed to a neighbouring province under different civil rule; His method, to preaching from place to place; His purpose, to working with individuals. There's a peculiar word used here by Matthew to tell of Jesus' departure from Judea to a province under a different civil ruler; "He withdrew." The word used implies going away because of danger threatening. We will run across it again and each time at a crisis point.

The leaders refused Jesus because He was not duly labelled. It seems to be a prevailing characteristic to want men labelled, especially a characteristic of those who make the labels. There is always an eager desire regarding a stranger to learn whom he represents, who have put their stamp upon him and accepted him. And if the label is satisfactory, he is accepted in the degree in which the label is accepted. Others are marked with a large interrogation point. Inherent worth has a slow time. But sure? Yes, but slow. Jesus bore no label whose words they could spell out or wanted to. They were a bit rusty in the language of worth. How knoweth this man letters, having never learned! He seems to know, to know surprisingly well. He seems keenly versed in the law, able quickly to turn the tables upon their catch questions. But then it can't be the real article of learning, because He hasn't been in our established schools. He has no sheepskin in a dead language with our learned doctors' names learnedly inscribed. How indeed! An upstart!!

Yet always to the earnest, sincere inquirer there was authority enough. In His acts, an open-minded doctor of the law could read the stamp of God's approval. The ear open to learn, not waxed up by self-seeking plans, or filled with gold dust, heard the voice of divine approval out of the clouds, or in His presence and acts.

The aggressive rejection.

Then came the second stage, the aggressive rejection. This is the plotting stage. Their hot passion is cooling now into a hardening purpose. This has been shaping itself under the surface for months. Now it is open. This was a crowded year for Jesus, and a year of crowds. The Galileans had been in His southern audiences many a time and seen His miracles. The news of His coming up north to their country swiftly spread everywhere. The throngs are so great that the towns and villages are blockaded, and Jesus has recourse to the fields, where the people gather in untold thousands.

An ominous incident occurs at the very beginning of this Galilean work. It is a fine touch of character that Jesus at once pays a visit to His home village. One always thinks more of Him for that. He never forgot the home folk. The synagogue service on the Sabbath day gathers the villagers together. Jesus takes the teacher's place, and reads, from Isaiah, a bit of the prophecy of the coming One. Then with a rare graciousness and winsomeness that wins all hearts, and fastens every eye upon Himself, He begins talking of the fulfilment of that word in Himself.

Then there comes a strange, quick revulsion of feeling. Had some Jerusalem spy gotten in and begun his poisoning work already? Eyes begin to harden and jaws become set. "Why, that is the man that made our cattle-yoke." – "Yes, and fixed our kitchen table." – "He – the Messiah!" Then words of rebuke gently spoken, but with truth's razor edge. Then a hot burst of passion, and He is hustled out to the jagged edge of the hill to be thrown over. Then that wondrous presence awing them back, as their hooked hands lose hold, and their eyes again fasten with wonder, and He passed quietly on His way undisturbed. Surely that was the best evidence of the truth of His despised word.

Seven outstanding incidents here reveal the ever-hardening purpose of the leaders against Jesus. First comes another clash in the temple. Their ideas of what was proper on the Sabbath day receive a shock because a man enslaved by disease for years was healed with a word from Jesus' lips. Could there be a finer use of a Sabbath day! We can either think them really shocked, or hunting for a religious chance to fight Him. Jesus' reply seems so to enrage that a passion to kill Him grips them. It is notable that they had no doubt of the extent of Jesus' claim; "He called God His Own Father, making Himself equal with God." On these two things, His use of the Sabbath, and His claim of divinity, is based the aggressive campaign begun that day.

The incident draws from Him the marvellous words preserved by John in his fifth chapter. In support of His claim He quietly brings forward five witnesses, John His herald, His own miraculous acts, His Father, the Scriptures entrusted to their care, and Moses, the founder of the nation. That was a great line of testimony. This first thought of killing Him seems to have been a burst of hot, passionate rage, but gradually we shall find it cooled into a hardened, deliberate purpose.

At once Jesus returns to the northern province. And now they begin to follow Him up, and spy upon His movements and words. In Capernaum, His northern headquarters, a man apparently at unrest in soul about his sins, and palsied in body, is first assured of forgiveness, and then made bodily whole. Their criticism of His forgiving sins is silenced by the power evidenced in the bodily healing. But their plan of campaign is now begun in earnest, and is evident at once. Later criticism of His personal conduct and habits with the despised classes is mingled with an attempt to work upon His disciples and undermine their loyalty. The Sabbath question comes up again through the disciples satisfying their hunger in the grain fields, and brings from Jesus the keen comment that man wasn't made for the Sabbath, but to be helped through that day, and then the statement that must have angered them further that He was "Lord of the Sabbath."

Another Sabbath day in the synagogue they were on hand to see if He would heal a certain man with a withered hand whom they had gotten track of, "that they might accuse Him." They were spying out evidence for the use of the Jerusalem leaders. To His grief they harden their hearts against His plea for saving a man, a life, as against a tradition. And as the man with full heart and full eyes finds his chance of earning a living restored, they rush out, and with the fire spitting from their eyes, and teeth gritting, they plan to get their political enemies, the Herodian's, to help them kill Jesus. A number of these incidents give rise to these passionate outbursts to kill, which seem to cool off, but to leave the remnants that hardened into the cool purpose most to be dreaded.

A second time occurs that significant word, "withdrew." Jesus withdrew to the sea, followed by a remarkable multitude of Galileans, and others from such distant points as Tyre and Sidon on the north, Idumea on the extreme south, beyond the Jordan on the east, and from Jerusalem. He was safe with this sympathizing crowd.

The crowds were so great, and the days so crowded, that Jesus' very eating was interfered with. His friends remonstrate, and even think Him unduly swayed by holy enthusiasm. But it is a man come down from Jerusalem who spread freely among the crowds the ugly charge that He was in league with the devil, possessed by an unclean spirit, and that that explained His strange power. No uglier charge could be made. It reveals keenly the desperate purpose of the Jerusalem leaders. Clearly it was made to influence the crowds. They were panic-stricken over these crowds. What could He not do with such a backing, if He chose! Such a rumour would Spread like wildfire. Jesus shows His leadership. He at once calls the crowds about Him, speaks openly of the charge, and refutes it, showing the evident absurdity of it.

Then a strange occurrence takes place. While He is teaching a great crowd one day, there is an interruption in the midst of His speaking. Oddly, it comes from His mother and her other sons. They send in a message asking to see Him at once. This seems very strange. It would seem probable from the narrative that they had access to Him constantly. Why this sudden desire by the one closest to Him by natural ties to break into His very speaking for a special interview? Had these Jerusalem men been working upon the fears of her mother heart for the safety of her Son? She would use her influence to save Him from possible danger threatening? There is much in the incident to give colour to such a supposition. Perhaps a man of such fineness as He could be checked back by consideration for His mother's feelings. They were quite capable of pulling any wire to shut Him up, however ignorant they showed themselves of the simple sturdiness of true character. But the same man who so tenderly provides for His mother in the awful pain of hanging on a cross reminds her now that a divine errand is not to be hindered by nature's ties; that clear vision of duty must ever hold the reins of the heart.

Then comes the most terrible, and most significant event, up to this time, in the whole gospel narrative – the murder of John. This marks the sharpest crisis yet reached. For a year or so John had been kept shut up in a prison dungeon, evidence of his own faithfulness, and of the low moral tone, or absence of moral tone, of the time. Then one night there is a prolonged, debased debauchery in a magnificent palace; the cunning, cruel scheme of the woman whose wrong relation to Herod John had honestly condemned. The dancing young princess, the drunken oath, the terrible request, the glowing-coal eyes closed, the tongue that held crowds with its message of sin, and of the coming One stilled, the King's herald headless – the whole horrible, nightmare story comes with the swiftness of aroused passion, the suddenness of a lightning flash, the cold cruelty of indulged lust.

Instantly on getting the news Jesus "withdrew" – for the third time withdrew to a retired desert place. This had tremendous personal meaning for Him. Nothing has occurred thus far that spells out for Him the coming tragic close so large, so terribly large, as does this. He stays away from the Passover Feast occurring at this time, the only one of the four of His public career He failed to attend.

The murderous rejection.

This crisis leads at once into the final stage, the murderous rejection. Jesus is now a fugitive from the province of Judea, because the death plot has been deliberately settled upon. The southern leaders begin a more vigorous campaign of harrying Him up in Galilee. A fresh deputation of Pharisees come up from Jerusalem to press the fighting. They at once bring a charge against Jesus' disciples of being untrue to the time-honoured traditions of the national religion. Yet it is found to be regarding such trivial things as washing their hands and arms clear up to the elbows each time before eating, and of washing of cups and pots and the like. Jesus sharply calls attention to their hypocrisy and cant[12], by speaking of their dishonouring teachings and practices in matters of serious moment. Then He calls the crowd together and talks on the importance of being clean inside, in the heart and thought. Before all the crowds He calls them hypocrites. It's a sharp clash and break. Jesus at once "withdrew." It is the fourth time that significant danger word is used. This time His withdrawal is clear out of the Jewish territory, far up north to the vicinity of Tyre and Sidon, on the seacoast, and there He attempts to remain unknown.

After a bit He returns again, this time by a round-about way, to the Sea of Galilee. Quickly the crowds find out His presence and come; and again many a life and many a home are utterly changed by His touch. With the crowd come the Pharisees, this time in partnership with another group, the Sadducees, whom they did not love especially. They hypocritically beg a sign from heaven, as though eager to follow a divinely sent messenger. But He quickly discerns their purpose to tempt Him into something that can be used against Him. The sign is refused. Jesus never used His power to show that He could, but only to help somebody.

The fall of that year found Him boldly returning to the danger zone of Jerusalem for attendance on the harvest-home festival called by them the Feast of Tabernacles. It was the most largely attended of the three annual gatherings, attracting thousands of faithful Jews from all parts of the world. The one topic of talk among the crowds was Jesus, with varying opinions expressed; but those favourable to Him were awed by the keen purpose of the leaders to kill Him. When the festival was in full swing, one morning, Jesus quietly appears among the temple crowds,

---

[12] hypocritical and sanctimonious talk, typically of a moral, religious, or political nature.

and begins teaching. The leaders tried to arrest Him, but are held back by some hidden influence, nobody seeming willing to take the lead. Then the clique of chief priests send officers to arrest Him. But they are so impressed by His presence and His words, that they come back empty-handed, to the disgust of their superiors. Great numbers listening believe on Him, but some of the leaders, mingling in the crowd, stir up discussion so sharp that with hot passion, and eyes splashing green light, they stoop down and pick up stones to hurl at Him and end His life at once. It is the first attempt at personal violence in Jerusalem. But again that strange restraining power, and Jesus passes out untouched.

As he quietly passes through and out, He stops to give sight to a blind man. Interestingly enough it occurs on a Sabbath day. Instantly the leaders seize on this, and have a time of it with the man and his parents in turn, with this upshot, that the man for his bold confession of faith in Jesus is shut out from all synagogue privileges, in accordance with a decision already given out. He becomes an outcast, with all that that means. It's a fine touch that Jesus hunts up this outcast and gives him a free entrance into His own circle.

After this feast-visit to Jerusalem, Jesus probably returns to Galilee, as after previous visits there, and then one day leads His band of disciples up to the neighbourhood of snow-capped Hermon. Here probably occurs the transfiguration, the purpose of which was to tie up these future leaders of His, against the events now hurrying on with such swift pace. From this time begins the preparation of this inner circle for the coming tragedy so plain to His eyes.

Then begins that memorable last journey from Galilee toward Jerusalem through the country on the east of the Jordan. With marvellous boldness and courage, He steadfastly set His face toward Jerusalem. The ever-tightening grip of His purpose is in the set of His face. The fire burning so intensely within is in His eye as He tramps along the road alone, with the disciples following, awestruck and filled with wondering fear. Thirty-five deputations of two each are sent ahead into all the villages to be visited by Him. What an intense campaigner was Jesus! He was thoroughly, systematically stumping the whole country for God.

As He approaches nearer to the Jerusalem section the air gets tenser and hotter. The leaders are constantly harrying His steps, tempting with catch questions, seeking signs, poisoning the crowds – mosquito warfare! He moves steadily, calmly on. Some of the keenest things He said flashed out through the friction of contact with them. A tempting lawyer's question brings out the beautiful Samaritan parable. The old Sabbath question provokes a fresh tilt with a synagogue ruler. There is a cunning attempt by the Pharisees to get Him out of Herod's territory into their own. How intense the situation grew is graphically told in Luke's words, they "began to set themselves vehemently against Him, and to provoke Him to speak many things; laying wait for Him to catch something out of His mouth."

Though unmoved by the cunning effort of the Pharisees to get Him over from Herod's jurisdiction into Judea, despite their threatening attitude, the winter Feast of Dedication finds Him again in Jerusalem walking in one of the temple areas. Instantly He is surrounded by a group of these Jerusalem Jews who, with an air of apparent earnest inquiry, keep prodding Him with the request to be told plainly if He is really the Christ. His patient reply brings a storm of stones – almost. Held in check for a while by an invisible power, or by the power of His presence shown under such circumstances so often, again they attempt to seize His person, and again He seems invisibly to hold their hands back, as He quietly passes on His way out of their midst.

Then comes the stupendous raising of Lazarus, which brings faith in Him to great numbers, and results in the formal official decision of the national council to secure His death. He is declared a fugitive with a price set upon His head. Anybody knowing of His whereabouts must report the fact to the authorities. This decides Him not to show Himself openly among them. In a few weeks the pilgrims are crowding Jerusalem for the Passover. Jesus' name is on every tongue. The rumour that He was over the hills in Bethany takes a crowd over there, not simply to see Him, but to see the resurrected Lazarus. Then it was determined to kill Lazarus off, too.

That tremendous last week now begins. Jesus is seen to be the one masterly figure in the week's events. In comparison with His calm steady movements, these leaders run scurrying around, here and there, like headless hens. The week begins with the most public, formal presentation of Himself in a kingly fashion to the nation. It is their last chance. How wondrously patient and considerate is this Jesus! And how sublimely heroic! Into the midst of those men ravenous for His blood He comes. Seated with fine, unconscious majesty on a kingly beast, surrounded by ever-increasing multitudes loudly singing and speaking praises to God, over paths bestrewed with garments and branches of living green, slowly He mounts the hill road toward the city.

At a turn in the road all of a sudden the city lies spread out before Him. "He saw the city and wept over it."

"He sat upon the ass's colt and rode
Toward Jerusalem. Beside Him walked
Closely and silently the faithful twelve,
And on before Him went a multitude
Shouting hosannas, and with eager hands
Strewing their garments thickly in the way.
Th' unbroken foal beneath Him gently stepped,
Tame as its patient dam; and as the song
Of 'Welcome to the Son of David' burst
Forth from a thousand children, and the leaves
Of the waving branches touched its silken ears,
It turned its wild eye for a moment back,
And then, subdued by an invisible hand,
Meekly trod onward with its slender feet.

'The dew's last sparkle from the grass had gone
As He rode up Mount Olivet. The woods
Threw their cool shadows directly to the west;
And the light foal, with quick and toiling step,
And head bent low, kept up its unslackened way
Till its soft mane was lifted by the wind
Sent o'er the mount from Jordan. As He reached
The summit's breezy pitch, the Saviour raised
His calm blue eye – there stood Jerusalem!
Eagerly He bent forward, and beneath
His mantle's passive folds a bolder line
Than the wont slightness of His perfect limbs
Betrayed the swelling fulness of His heart.
There stood Jerusalem! How fair she looked –
The silver sun on all her palaces,
And her fair daughters 'mid the golden spires
Tending their terrace flowers; and Kedron's stream
Lacing the meadows with its silver band
And wreathing its mist-mantle on the sky
With the morn's exhalation. There she stood,
Jerusalem, the city of His love,

Chosen from all the earth: Jerusalem,
That knew Him not, and had rejected Him;
Jerusalem for whom He came to die!

"The shouts redoubled from a thousand lips
At the fair sight; the children leaped and sang
Louder hosannas; the clear air was filled
With odor from the trampled olive leaves
But 'Jesus wept!' The loved disciple saw
His Master's tear, and closer to His side
He came with yearning looks, and on his neck
The Saviour leaned with heavenly tenderness,
And mourned, 'How oft, Jerusalem! would I
Have gathered you, as gathereth a hen
Her brood beneath her wings – but ye would not!'

"He thought not of the death that He should die –
He thought not of the thorns He knew must pierce
His forehead – of the buffet on the cheek –
The scourge, the mocking homage, the foul scorn!

"Gethsemane stood out beneath His eye
Clear in the morning sun; and there, He knew,
While they who 'could not watch with Him one hour'
Were sleeping, He should sweat great drops of blood,
Praying the cup might pass! And Golgotha
Stood bare and desert by the city wall;
And in its midst, to His prophetic eye
Rose the rough cross, and its keen agonies
Were numbered all – the nails were in His feet –
Th' insulting sponge was pressing on His lips –
The blood and water gushed from His side –
The dizzy faintness swimming in His brain –
And, while His own disciples fled in fear,
A world's death agonies all mixed in His!
Ah! – He forgot all this. He only saw
Jerusalem – the chosen – the loved – the lost!
He only felt that for her sake His life
Was vainly given, and in His pitying love
The sufferings that would clothe the heavens in black

And so the King entered His capital. It was a royal procession. Mark keenly the result. Again that utter, ominous, loud silence, that greeted His ears first, more than three years before. He had come to His own home. His own kinsfolk received Him not!

Then each day He came to the city, and each night, homeless, slept out in the open, under the trees of Olivet, and the blue. Now, He rudely shocks them by clearing the temple areas of the market-place rabble and babble, and now He is healing the lame and maimed in the temple itself, amid the reverent praise of the multitude, the songs of the children, and the scowling, muttered protests of the chief priests. Calmly, day by day, He moves among them, while their itching fingers vainly clutch for a hold upon Him, and as surely are held back by some invisible force. By every subtle device known to cunning, crafty men, they lay question-traps, and lie in wait to catch His word. He foils them with His marvellous, simple answers, lashes them with His keen, cutting parables and finally Himself proposes a question about their own scriptures which they admit themselves unable to answer, and, utterly defeated, ask no more questions. Then follows that most terrific arraignment[14] of these leaders, with its infinitely tender, sad, closing lament over Jerusalem. That is the final break.

Then occurs that pathetic Greek incident that seems to agitate Jesus so. This group of earnest seekers, from the outside, non-Jewish world brings to Jesus a vision of the great hungry heart of the world, and of an open-mindedness to truth such as was to Him these days as a cool, refreshing drink to a dusty mouth on a dry hot day. But – no – the Father's will – simple obedience – only that was right. The harvest can come only through the grain giving out its life in the cold ground.

Before the final act in the tragedy Jesus retires from sight, probably for prayer. Some dear friends of Bethany in whose home He had rested many a time, where He ever found sweet-sympathy, arranged a little

---

[13] Nathaniel Parker Willis

[14] Arraignment - Arraignment is a formal reading of a criminal charging document in the presence of the defendant to inform the defendant of the charges against them. In response to arraignment, the accused is expected to enter a plea.

home-feast for Him where a few congenial friends might gather. While seated there in the quiet atmosphere of love and fellowship so grateful to Him after those Jerusalem days, one of the friends present, a woman, Mary, takes a box of exceeding costly ointment, and anoints His head. To the strange protests made, Jesus quietly explains her thought in the act. She alone understood what was coming. Alone of all others it was a woman, the simple-hearted Bethany Mary, who understood Jesus. As none other did she perceive with her keen love-eyes the coming death, and – more – its meaning.

It is one of the disciples, Judas, who protests indignantly against such waste. This ointment would have brought at least seventy-five dollars, and how much such a sum would have done for the poor! Thoughtless, improvident woman! Strange the word didn't blister on his canting lips. John keenly sees that his fingers are clutching the treasure bag as he speaks the word, and that his thoughts are far from the poor. Jesus gently rebukes Judas. But Judas is hot tempered, and sullenly watches for the first chance to withdraw and carry out the damnable purpose that has been forming within. He hurries over the hill, through the city gate, up to the palace of the chief priest.

Within there was a company of the inner clique of the leaders, discussing how to get hold of Jesus most easily. They sit heavily in their seats, with shut fists, set jaws, and that peculiar yellow-green light spitting out from under their lowering, knit brows. These bothersome crowds had to be considered. The feast-day wouldn't do. The crowd would be greatest then, and hardest to handle. Back and forth they brew their scheme. Then a knock at the door. Startled, they look alertly up to know who this intruder may be. The door is opened. In steps a man with a hangdog, guilty, but determined look. It is one of the men they have seen with Jesus! What can this mean? He glances furtively from one to another.

Then he speaks: "How much'll you give if I get Jesus into your hands?" Of all things this was probably the last they had thought might happen. Their eyes gleam. How much indeed – a good snug sum to get their fingers securely on his person. But they're shrewd bargainers. That's one of their specialties. How much did he want? Poor Judas! He made a bad bargain that day. Thirty pieces of silver! He could easily have gotten a thousand. Judas did love money greedily, and doubtless was a good bargainer too, but anger was in the saddle now, and drove him hard. Without doubt it was in a hot fit of temper that he made this proposal. His descendants have been coining money out of Jesus right along: exchanging Him for gold.

Only a little later, and the Master is closeted with His inner circle in the upper room of a faithful friend's house in one of the Jerusalem streets, for the Passover supper. A word from Him and Judas withdraws for his dark errand. Then those great heart-talks of Jesus, in the upper room, along the roadway, under the full moon, maybe passing by the massive temple structure, then under the olive trees. Then the hour grows late, the disciples are drowsy, the Master is off alone among those trees, then weird uncertain lights of torches, a rabble of soldiers and priests, a man using friendship's cloak, and friendship's greeting – then the King is in the hands of His enemies. An awful night, followed by a yet more awful day, and the plan of the kingdom is broken by the tragic killing of the King.

Suffering the birth-pains of a new life.

Why did Jesus die? It's a pretty old question. It's been threshed out no end of times. Yet every time one thinks of the gospel, or opens the Book, it looks out earnestly into his face. And nothing is better worthwhile than to have another serious prayerful go at it. The whole nub of the gospel is here. It clears the ground greatly not to have any theory about Jesus' death, but simply to try thoughtfully to gather up all the statements and group them, regardless of where it may lead, or how it may knock out previous ideas.

It can be said at once that His dying was not God's own plan. It was a plan conceived somewhere else, and yielded to by God. God had a plan of atonement by which men who were willing could be saved from sin and its effects. That plan is given in the old Hebrew code. To the tabernacle, or temple, under prescribed regulations, a man could bring some live animal which he owned. The man brought that which was his own. It represented him. Through his labour the beast or bird was his. He had transferred some of his life and strength into it. He identified himself with it further by close touch at the time of its being offered. He offered up its life. In his act he acknowledged that his own life was forfeited. In continuing to live he acknowledged the continued life as belonging to God. He was to live as belonging to another. He made, in effect, the statement made long after by Paul: "I am offering up my life on this altar for my sin; nevertheless, I am living: yet the life I live is no longer mine, but another's. Mine has been taken away by sin."

There was no malice or evil feeling in the man's act, but only penitence, and an earnest, noble purpose.

The act revealed the man's inner spirit. It acknowledged his sin, that life is forfeited by sin, his desire to have the sin difficulty straightened out, and to be at one again with God. He expressed his hatred of sin and his earnest desire to be free of it. I am not saying at all that this was true of every Hebrew coming with his sacrifice. I may not say it of all who approach God to day through Jesus. But clearly enough, all of this is in the old Hebrew plan devised by God. It was the new choice that brought the man back to God, even as the first choice had separated him from God. And the explicit statement made over and over is this, "and it shall make atonement."

Clearly Jesus' dying does not in any way fit into the old Hebrew form of sacrifice, nor into the spirit of the man who caused the death of the sacrifice, though in spirit, in requirement it far more than fills it out. The Old Testament scheme is Jewish. The manner of Jesus' death is not Jewish, but Roman. As a priest He was not of the Jewish order, but of an order non-Jewish and antedating the other by hundreds of years. In no feature does He fit into the old custom. But every truth taught by the old is brilliantly exemplified and embodied in Him.

The epistle to the Hebrews was written to Jews who had become Christians, but through persecution and great suffering were sorely tempted to go back to the old Jewish faith. They seemed to be saying that Jesus filled out neither the kingdom plan, nor the Mosaic scheme of sacrifice. The writer of the epistle is showing with a masterly sweep and detail the immense superiority of what Jesus did over the old Mosaic plan. Read backward, these provisions are seen to be vivid illustrations of what Jesus did do, not in form, not actually, but in fact, in spirit, in a way vastly ahead of the Hebrew ritual. The truth underneath the old was fully fulfilled in Jesus, though the form was not.

One needs always to keep sharply in mind the difference between God's plan and that which He clearly saw ahead, and into which He determined to fit in carrying out His purpose. There is no clearer, stronger statement of this than that found in Peter's Pentecost sermon: "Him being delivered up by the determinate counsel and foreknowledge of God, ye by the hands of men without law did crucify and slay." God knew ahead what would come. There was a conference held. The whole matter talked over. With full knowledge of the situation, the obstinate hatred of men, the terrific suffering involved, it was calmly, resolutely advised and decided upon that when the time came Jesus should yield Himself up pliantly into their hands. That is Peter's statement.

This in no way affects the fact that Jesus dying as He did is the one means of salvation. It does not at all disturb any of Paul's statements, in their plainest, first-flush meaning. It does explain the kingdom plan, and the necessity for Jesus finishing up the kingdom plan someday. For though God's plan may be broken, and retarded, it always is carried through in the end. It explains too that evil is never necessary to good. Hatred, evil never helps God's plans. The good that God brought out of the cross is not through the bad, but in spite of the bad.

The preaching of the Acts is absorbed with the astounding, overshadowing, appalling fact of the killing of the nation's King. But through it all runs this strain of reasoning: the kingdom plan has been broken by the murder of the King. He has been raised from the dead in vindication of His claim. This marvellous power that is so evident to all eyes and ears is the Holy Spirit whom the killed King has sent down. It proves that He is now enthroned in glory at God's right hand. He is coming back to carry out the kingdom plan. Now the thing to do is to repent, and so there will come blessing now, and by and by the King again.

When the first church council is held to discuss the matter of letting non-Jewish outsiders into their circle, the clear-headed, judicial-tempered James, in the presiding chair, puts the thing straight. He says: "Peter has fully told us how God first visited the outside nations to take out of them a people for Himself. And this fits into the prophetic plan as outlined by Amos, that after that the kingdom will be set up and then all men will come."

This brings out in bold relief the fact that the horrible features of Jesus' dying, the hatred and cruelty, were no part of the plan of salvation, and not necessary to the plan. The cross was the invention of hate. There is no cross in God's plan of atonement. It is the superlative degree of hate, brooded and born, and grown lusty in hell. It was God's master touch that, through yielding, it becomes to all men for all time the superlative degree of love. The ages have softened all its sharp jagged edges with a halo of glory.

It is perfectly clear, too, that Jesus died of His own accord. He chose the time of His death and the manner of it. He had said it was purely voluntary on His part, and the record plainly shows that it was. All attempts to kill Him failed until He chose to yield. There are ten separate mentions of their effort, either to get hold of His person or to kill Him at once before they finally succeeded. He was killed in intent at least three times, once by being dashed over a precipice, and twice by stoning, before He was actually killed by crucifixion. Each time surrounded by a hostile crowd, apparently quite capable of doing as they pleased, yet each time He passes through their midst, and their hooked fingers are restrained against their will, and their gnashing teeth bite only upon the spittle of their hate.

This makes Jesus' motive in yielding explain His death. The cross means just what His purpose in dying puts into it. If we read the facts of the gospel stories apart from Jesus' words, the cross spells out just one word – in large, pot-black capitals – HATE.

What was Jesus' motive or purpose in dying? His own words give the best answer. The earlier remarks are obscure to those who heard, not understood. And we can understand that they could not. At the first Passover He speaks of their destroying "this temple," and His raising it in three days. Naturally they think of the building of stone, but He is thinking of His body. To Nicodemus He says that the Son of Man must "be lifted up": and to some critics that when the "bridegroom" is "taken away" there will be fasting among His followers.

Later, He speaks much more plainly. After John has gone home by way of Herod's red road, at the time of the feeding of the 5,000 there is the discussion about bread, and the true bread. Jesus speaks a word that perplexes the crowd much, and yet He goes on to explain just what He means. It is in John, sixth chapter, verses fifty-three to fifty-seven inclusive, He says that if a man eat His flesh and drink His blood he shall have eternal life. The listening crowd takes the words literally and of course is perplexed. Clearly enough it is not meant to be taken literally. Read in the light of the after events it is seen to be an allusion to His coming death. Such a thing as actually eating His flesh and drinking His blood would necessitate His death.

We men are under doom of death written in our very bodies, assured to us by the unchangeable fact of bodily death. Now if a man takes Jesus into his very being so that they become one in effect, then clearly if Jesus die the man is freed from the necessity of dying. Through Jesus dying there is for such a man life. That is the statement Jesus makes.

In five distinct sentences He attempts to make His meaning simple and clear. The first sentence puts the negative side: there is no life without Jesus being taken into one's being. Then the positive side: through this sort of eating there is life. And with this is coupled the inferential statement that they are not to be spared bodily death, because they are to be raised up. The third sentence, that Jesus is the one true food of real life. The fourth sentence gives a parallel or interchangeable phrase for eating and drinking, i.e., "abideth in me and I in Him." A mutual abiding in each other. The food abides in the man eating it. The man abides in the strength of the food He has taken in. Eating My flesh means abiding in Me. The last sentence gives an illustration. This living in Jesus, having Him live in us as closely as though actually eaten, is the same as Jesus' own life on earth being lived in His Father, dependent upon the Father. And when the crowds take His words literally and complain that none can understand such statements, He at once explains that, of course, He does not mean literal eating – "The flesh profiteth nothing" (even if you did eat it): "it is the Spirit that gives life:" "the words ... are Spirit and life." The taking of Jesus through His words into one's life to dominate – that is the meaning.

A few months later, in Jerusalem, He speaks again of His purpose, in John's tenth chapter, "The good shepherd layeth down His life for the sheep." "I lay down my life for the sheep." The death was for others because of threatening danger. "Other sheep I have which are not of this fold: them also I must lead." Here is clear foresight of the wide sweep of influence through His death. "I lay down my life that I may take it again." The death was one step in a plan. There is something beyond. "I lay it down of myself. I have the right to lay it down, and I have the right to take it again. This commandment I received from my Father." The dying was voluntary and was agreed to between the Father and Himself. To the disciples He speaks of the need of taking up a "cross" in order to be followers, and to the critical Pharisee asking a sign, He alludes to Jonah's three days and nights in the belly of the sea monster. Neither of these allusions conveyed any definite idea to those listening.

Then the last week when the Greeks came; "Except a grain of wheat fall into the earth and die, it abideth by itself alone; but if it die, it beareth much fruit." The dying was to have great influence upon others. "And I if I be lifted up from the earth will draw all men unto myself." The dying was to be for others, and to exert tremendous influence upon the whole race.

In that last long talk with the eleven, "that the world may know that I love the Father and as the Father gave me commandment even so I do." The dying was in obedience to His Father's wish, and was to let men know of the great love between Father and Son. "Greater love hath no man than this, that a man lay down his life for his friends." This dying was for these friends. And in that great prayer that lays His heart bare, "for their sakes I sanctify myself that they also may be sanctified in truth." The dying is for others, and is for the securing in these others of a certain spirit or character. The reference to the dying being in accord with the Father's wish comes out again at the arrest, "The cup that the Father hath given me, shall I not drink it?"

To these quotations from Jesus' lips may be added a significant one from the man who stood closest to Jesus. Referring to a statement about Jesus made by Caiaphas, John adds: "being high priest that year he prophesied that Jesus should die for the nation; and not for the nation only, but that He might gather together into one the children of God that are scattered abroad." As John understood the matter, the death was not simply for others, but for the Jewish nation as a nation, and beyond that for a gathering into one of all of God's children. Jesus was to be God's magnet for attracting together all that belong to Him. The death was to be a roadway through to something beyond.

From His own words, then, Jesus saw a necessity for His dying. He "must" be lifted up. That "must" spells out the desperateness of the need and the strength of His love. Sin contains in itself death for man as a logical result. And by death is not meant the passing of life out of the body. That is a mere incident of death. Death is separation from God. It is gradual until finally complete. Love would plan nothing less radical than a death that would be for man the death of death. His death was to be for others, it was purely voluntary, it was by agreement with His Father, in obedience to His wishes, and an evidence of His filial love. The death is a step in a plan. There is something beyond, growing out of the death.

Jesus plans not merely a transfer of the death item, but a new life, a new sort of life, in its place. The dying is but a step. It is a great step, tremendously great, indispensable, the step that sets the pace. Yet but one step of a number. Beyond the dying is the living, living a new life. He works out in Himself the plan for them – a dying, and after that a new life, and a new sort of life. Then according to His other teaching there is the sending of some One else to men to work out in His name in each of them this plan. That plan is to be worked out in each man choosing to receive Him into his life. He will send down His other self, the Holy Spirit, to work this out in each one. Jesus' death released His life to be re-lived in us. Jesus plans to get rid of the sin in a man, and put in something else in its place. The sin must be gotten out, first washed out, then burned out. Then a new seed put in that will bear life. What a chemist and artist in one is this Jesus! He uses bright red, to get a pure white out of a dead black.

In addition to the plan for man individually, the dying is to produce the same result in the Jewish nation. There is to be a national new-birth. A new Jewish people. And then the dying is to have a tremendous influence upon all men. On the cross Jesus would suffer the birth-pains of a new life for man and for the world. Such, in brief, seems to be the grouping of Jesus' own thought about His dying. Its whole influence is towards man.

The value of Jesus' dying lies wholly in its being voluntary. Of deliberate purpose He allowed them to put Him to death. Otherwise they could not, as is fully proven by their repeated failures. And the purpose as well as the value of the death lies entirely in His motive in yielding. If they could have taken His life without His consent, then that death would have been an expression of their hate, and only that. But as it is, it forever stands an expression of two things. On their part of the intensest, hottest hate; on His part of the finest, strongest love. It makes new records for both hate and love. Sin put Jesus to death. In yielding to these men Jesus was yielding to sin, for they personified sin. And sin yielded to quickly brought death, its logical outcome.

Jesus' dying being His own act, controlled entirely by His own intention, makes it sacrificial. There are certain necessary elements in such a sacrifice. It must be voluntary. It must involve pain or suffering of some sort. The suffering must be undeserved, that is, in no way or degree a result of one's own act, else it is not sacrifice, but logical result. It must be for others. And the suffering must be of a sort that would not come save for this voluntary act. It must be supposed to bring benefit to the others. Each of these elements must be in to make up fully a sacrifice. There are elements of sacrifice in much noble suffering by man. But in no one do all of these elements perfectly combine and blend, save in Jesus.

To this agree the words of the philosopher of the New Testament writers. It would be so, of course, for the Spirit of Jesus swayed Paul. The epistle to the Romans contains a brief packed summary of his understanding of the gospel plan. There is in it one remarkable statement of the Father's, purpose in Jesus' death. In the third chapter, verse twenty-six, freely translated, "that He might be reckoned righteous in reckoning righteous the man who has faith." "That He might be reckoned righteous" – that is, in His attitude toward sin. That in allowing things to go on as they were, in holding back sin's logical judgment, He was not careless or indifferent about sin or making light of it. He was controlled by a great purpose.

God's great difficulty was to make clear at once both His love and His hate: His love for man: His hate for the sin that man had grained in so deep that they were as one. For the man's sake He must show His love to win and change him. For man's sake He must show His hate of sin that man, too, might know its hatefulness and learn to hate it with intensest hate. His love for man is to be the measure of man's hate for sin. The death of Jesus was God's master-stroke. At one stroke He told man His estimate of man and His estimate of man's sin; His love and His hate. It was the measureless measure of His hate for sin, and His love for man. It was a master-stroke too, in that He took sin's worst – the cross – and in it revealed His own best. Out of what was meant for God's defeat, came sin's defeat, and God's greatest victory.

And the one simple thing that transfers to a man all that Jesus has worked out for him is what is commonly called "faith." That is, trusting God, turning the heart Godward, yielding to the inward upward tug, letting the pleasing of God dominate the life. This, be it keenly marked, has ever been the one simple condition in every age and in every part of the earth.

Abraham believed God and it was reckoned to him for righteousness. The devout Hebrew, reverently, penitently standing with his hand on the head of his sacrifice, at the tabernacle door, believed God and it was reckoned to him for righteousness. The devout heathen with face turned up to the hill top, and feet persistently toiling up, patiently seeking glory and honour and incorruption believes God, though he may not know His name, and it is reckoned to him for righteousness. The devout Christian, with his hand in Christ's, believes God, and it is counted to him for righteousness.

The devout Hebrew, the earnest heathen, and the more enlightened believer in Jesus group themselves here by the common purpose that grips them alike. The Hebrew with his sacrifice, the heathen with his patient continuance, and the Christian who knows more in knowing Jesus, stand together under the mother wing of God.

Some Surprising Results of the Tragic Break

The surprised Jew.

God proposes. Man disposes. God proposed a king, and a world-wide kingdom with great prosperity and peace. Man disposed of that plan for the bit of time and space controlled by his will, and in its place interposed for the king, a cross. Out of such a radical clashing of two great wills have come some most surprising results.

The first surprise was for the Jew. Within a few weeks after Jesus' final departure, Jerusalem, and afterward Palestine, was filled with thousands of people believing in Him. A remarkable campaign of preaching starts up and sweeps everything before it. Jesus' name was on every tongue as never before. But there were earnest Jews who could not understand how Jesus could be the promised Messiah. He had not set up a kingdom. Their Scriptures were full of a kingdom.

The Jew, whether in their largest colony in Babylon, or in Jerusalem, or in Rome, or Alexandria, or the smaller colonies everywhere, was full of the idea, the hope, of a kingdom. He was absorbed with more or less confused and materialized, unspiritual ideas of a coming glory for his nation through a coming king. But among the followers of this Jesus there is something else coming into being, a new organization never even hinted at in their Scriptures. It is called the church. It is given a name that indicates that it is to be made up of persons taken out from among all nations.

There comes to be now a three-fold division of all men. There had been with the Jews, always, a two-fold division, the Jew and the Gentiles, or outside nations. Now three, the Jew, the outsiders, and the church. The church is an eclectic society, a chosen out body. Its principle of organization is radically different from that of the Hebrew nation. Their membership was by birth right. Here it is by individual choice and belief.

Foreigners coming in were not required to become Jews, as under the old, but remained essentially as they have been in all regards, except the one thing of relationship to Jesus in a wholly spiritual sense. There is constant talk about "the gospel of the kingdom," but the kingdom itself seems to have quite slipped away, and the church is in its place. Such a situation must have been very puzzling to any Jew. His horizon was full of a kingdom – a Jewish kingdom. Anything else was unthinkable. These intense Orientals could not conceive of anything else. It had taken a set of visions to swing Peter and the other church leaders into line even on letting outsiders into the church.

This Jesus does not fill out this old Hebrew picture of a king and a kingdom. How can He be the promised Messiah? This was to thousands a most puzzling question, and a real hindrance to their acceptance of Jesus, even by those profoundly impressed with the divine power being seen.

This was the very question that had puzzled John the Baptist those weary months, till finally he sends to Jesus for some light on his puzzle. Jesus fills out part of the plan, and splendidly, but only part, and may be what seems to some the smaller part. Can it be, John asks, that there is to be another one coming to complete the picture? To him Jesus does not give an answer, except that he must wait and trust. He would not in words anticipate the nation's final rejection, though so well He knew what was coming. Their chance was not yet run out for the acceptance of Jesus that would fill out John's picture. God never lets His foreknowledge influence one whit man's choice. It was a most natural and perplexing difficulty, both for John and later for these thousands.

The answer to all this has its roots down in that tragic break. In the old picture of the Messiah there are two distinct groups of characteristics of the coming king, personal and official. He was to have a direct personal relation to men and an official relation to the nation, and through it to the world. The personal had in it such matters as healing the sick, relieving the distressed, raising the dead, feeding the hungry, easing heart strains, teaching and preaching. It was wholly a personal service. The official had, of course, to do with establishing the great kingdom and bringing all other nations into subjection. Now, it was a bit of the degeneracy of the people and of the times, that when Jesus came the blessings to the individual had slipped from view, and that the national conception, grown gross and coarse, had seized upon the popular imagination, and was to the fore.

Jesus filled in perfectly with marvellous fullness the individual details of the prophetic picture. Of course filling in the national depended upon national acceptance, and failure there meant failure for that side. And, of course, He could not fill out the national part except through the nation's acceptance of Him as its king. Rejection there meant a breaking, a hindering of that part. And so Jesus does not fill out the old Hebrew picture of the Messiah. He could not without the nation's consent. Man would have used force to seize the national reins. But, of course, God's man could not do that. It would be against God's plan for man. Everything must be through man's consent.

Out of this perplexity there came to be the four Gospels. They grew up out of the needs of the people. Mark seems to have written his first. He makes a very simple recital, setting down the group of facts and sayings as He had heard Peter telling them in many a series of talks. It is the simplest of the four, aiming to tell what he had gotten from another. But it offers no answer to these puzzling questions.

Matthew writes his account of the gospel for these great numbers of perplexed, earnest Jewish questioners. They are Palestinian Jews, thoroughly familiar with Jewish customs and places. Sitting backward on the edge of the Hebrew past, thoroughly immersed in its literature and atmosphere, but with his face fastened on Jesus, he composes out of the facts about Jesus and the old prophetic scriptures a perfect bit of mosaic. There is the fascination of a serpent's eye in turning from the prophetic writings to the Gospel of Matthew. Let a man become immersed and absorbed in the vision of the Hebrew prophetic books and then turn to Matthew to get the intense impression that this promised One has come, at last has actually come, and – tragedy of tragedies – is being rejected.

This is the gap gospel. It bridges the gap between the prophetic books and the book of Acts, between the kingdom which has slipped out and the church which has come in. It explains the adjournment of the kingdom for a specified time, the church filling a sort of interregnum in the kingdom. The kingdom is to come later when the church mission is complete. It tells with great care and with convincing power that Jesus filled perfectly the prophecy of the Messiah in every detail personally, and did not fill out the national features because of the nation's unwillingness. That is the Matthew Gospel.

Paul was the apostle to the outside nations. His great work was outside of Palestine. He dealt with three classes, Jews, outsiders who in religious matters had allied themselves with the Jews, but without changing their nationality, and then the great outside majority, chiefly the great crowds of other nationalities. These people needed a gospel of their own. Their standpoint is so wholly different from the Jews' that Matthew's gospel does not suit, nor Mark's. Paul, through Peter and Barnabas and others, has absorbed the leading facts and teachings of those three years, and works them over for his non Jewish crowds. He omits much that would appeal peculiarly to Jews, and gives the setting and colouring that would be most natural to his audiences.

His studious companion, Doctor Luke, undertakes to write down this account of Jesus' life as Paul tells it, and for Paul's audience and territory, especially these great outside non-Jewish crowds of people. He goes to Palestine, and carefully studies and gathers up all the details and facts available. He adds much that the two previous writers had not included. One can easily understand his spending several days with Mary, the now aged mother of Jesus, in John's home in Jerusalem, and from her lips gleaning the exquisite account of the nativity of her divinely conceived Son. He largely omits names of places, for they would be unknown and not of value or interest. When needed, he gives explanation about places.

These three gospels follow one main line; they tell the story of the rejection of Jesus. Then there arose a generation that did not know Jesus, the Jesus that had tramped Jerusalem's streets and Galilee's roads. Some were wondering, possibly, how it was that these gospels are absorbed in telling of Jesus' rejection. There surely was a reason for it if He was so sweepingly rejected. So John in his old age writes. His chief thought is to show that from the first Jesus was accepted by individuals as well as rejected by the nation. These two things run neck and neck through his twenty-one chapters, along the pathway he makes of witnessed, established facts regarding Jesus. The nation – the small, powerfully entrenched group of men who held the nation's leadership in their tenacious fingers – the nation rejects. It's true. But the ugly reason is plain to all, even the Roman who gave final sentence. From the first, Jesus was accepted by men of all classes, including the most thoughtful and scholarly.

He is writing to the generation that has grown up since Jesus has gone, and so to all after generations that knew of Him first by hearing of Him. He is writing after the Jewish capital has been levelled to the ground, and the nation utterly destroyed as a nation, and to people away from Palestine. So he explains Jewish usages and words as well as places in Palestine, to make the story plain and vivid to all. And the one point at which he drives constantly is to make it clear to all after generations that men of every sort of Jesus' own generation believed; questioned, doubted, examined, weighed, believed, with whole-hearted loving loyalty followed this Jesus.

This decides the order in which, with such rare wisdom, the churchmen later arranged the four gospels in grouping the New Testament books. The order is that of the growth of the new faith of the church from the Jewish outward. Next to the Hebrew pages lies the gap gospel, then the earliest, simplest telling, then the outsiders' gospel, and then the gospel for after generations.

The surprised church.

Man proposes. God disposes. Man may for a time set aside God's plan, but through any series of contrary events God holds steadily to His own plan. Temporary defeat is only adjournment, paving the way for later and greater victory. Another surprise is for the church, that is, the church of later generations, including our own. The old Jew saw only a triumphant king, not a suffering king. He saw only a kingdom. There was no hint of any such thing as a church. The church to-day, and since the day of Constantine, sees only a church. The kingdom has merged into the church or slipped out of view.

There seems to be a confused mixing of church and kingdom, but always with the church the big thing, and the kingdom a sort of vague, indefinite – folks don't seem to know just what – an ideal, a spiritual conception, or something like that. The church is supposed to have taken the place of the kingdom. Its mission seems to be supposed to be the doing for the world what the kingdom was to do, but, being set aside, failed to do.

In reading the old Book there is a handy sort of explanation largely in use that applies all that can be fitted into the theory in hand, and calmly ignores or conveniently adjusts the rest. The Old Testament blessings for the Jewish kingdom are appropriated and applied to the church. The curses there are handed over to the Jews or ignored. There seems to be a plan of interpreting one part of the Bible one way and another part in a different way. This part is to be taken literally. This other not literally, spiritually, the only guiding principle being the man's preconceived idea of what should be. The air seems quite a bit foggy sometimes. A man has to go off for a bit of fresh air and get straightened out with himself inside.

A whiff of keen, sharp air seems needed to clear the fog and bring out the old outlines – a whiff? – a gale! Yet it must needs blow, like God's wind of grace always blows, as a soft gentle breeze. The common law among folk in all other matters for understanding any book or document is that some one rule of interpretation be applied consistently to all its parts. If we attempt to apply here the rule of first-flush, common sense meaning, as would be done to a house lease or an insurance policy, it brings out this surprising thing. The church is distinct from the kingdom. It came through the kingdom failing to come. It fits into a gap in the kingdom plan. It has a mission quite distinct from that of the kingdom.

The church is to complete its mission and go. The kingdom, in the plain meaning of the word kingdom, is to come, and be the dominant thing before the eyes of all men. The church goes up and out. The kingdom comes in and down. Later the church is to be a part of the executive of the kingdom. This seems to be the simple standpoint of the Book.

The tragic break does not hinder the working of the plan. It simply retards it awhile. A long while? Yes, to man, who counts time by the bulky measurement of years, and can't seem to shake off the time idea; who gets absorbed in moments and hours and loses the broad swing of things. To God? No. He lives in eternities, and reckons things by events. His eye never loses the whole, nor a single detail of the whole.

But yet more. That break leads to an enriching of the plan. Out of hate God reveals love. Not a greater love, but a greater opportunity for greatly revealing love. Man's unwillingness and opposition may delay God's plan, but cannot hinder it. A man can hinder it for his own self if he so insists. But for others he can only delay, not hinder. Though God may patiently yield His own plan, for a time, to something else, through which meanwhile His main purpose is being served, yet He never loses sight of His own plan – the highest expression of His love. And when He does so yield, it is that through the interruption He may in the long run work out the higher and the highest.

And so in the fulfilment of God's plan as given by His Hebrew spokesmen, there is a sort of sliding scale. A partial fulfilment takes place, leaving the full fulfilment for the full working out of the plan. The fulfilment takes place in two stages, the first being only less full than the final. Thus Elijah is to come. But first comes John, a man with most striking resemblance to Elijah. The outpouring of the Holy Spirit prophesied in Joel is to be upon all flesh. But before that takes place, comes the Pentecost outpouring, filling out the Joel prophecy in spirit, but not in the full measure.

As a matter of good faith the King must come back and carry out the kingdom plan in full. And judging simply by the character of God and of Jesus, I haven't a bit of doubt that He will do it. No amount of disturbance ever alters the love of God, nor His love-plan in the long run, however patiently He may bear with breaks.

Even this phase is in the minor strain of the old Hebrew. 'They shall look upon Him whom they have pierced; and they shall mourn for Him, as one mourneth for his only son." There is a future meeting of the rejected King and His rejecting people, and this time with sorrow for their former conduct, which implies different conduct at this meeting time. And to this agrees the whole swing of the New Testament teaching. Peter says the going away of Jesus is to be "until the restitution of all things." He is to return and carry out the old plan.

It's a bit unfortunate that some earnest, lovable people have pushed this phase of truth so much to the front as to get it out of its proportion in the whole circle of truth. Truth must always be kept in its place in the circle of truth. Truth is fact in right proportion. Out of that it begins to breed misstatement and error. Jesus' coming back is not to wind things up. It is to begin things anew. There will be certain phases of judgment, doubtless, a clearing of the deck for action, but no general judgment till long after. The kingdom is to swing to the front, and bring a new life to the earth for a very long time. Then after that the wind-up.

The gospel preached in the Acts is the "gospel of the kingdom." They are always expecting it to come. Paul constantly alludes to the Master's return as the great thing to look forward to, as distinctly at the close as at the beginning of his ministry. The book of Revelation is distinctly a kingdom book, and however it may, with the versatility of Scripture to serve a double purpose, foreshadow the characteristics of history for the centuries since its writing, plainly its first meaning has to do with the time when "the kingdom of the world is become the kingdom of our Lord and of His Christ." The King is coming back to straighten matters out, and organize a new running of things. This is the church's surprise, and a great surprise it will apparently be to a great many folks, though not to all.

The surprising Jew.

There is a third surprise growing out of this tragic break, the greatest of all – the Jew. The first surprises were for the Jew, the later surprise for the church; this surprise has been and is for all the world. The Jew has been the running puzzle of history. A strange, elusive, surprising puzzle he has been to historians and all others. Not a nation, only a people, flagless, without country, without any semblance of organization, they have been mixed in with all the peoples of the earth, yet always distinctly separate.

They have been persecuted, bitterly, cruelly, persistently persecuted, as no other people has ever been, yet with a power of recovery of none other too. With an astonishing vitality, resourcefulness, and leadership, they have taken front rank in every circle of life and every phase of activity, in art, music, science, commerce, philanthropy, statesmanship; holding the keys of government for great nations, of treasure boxes, and of exclusive social circles; making their own standards regardless of others, and with the peculiarity of strongest leadership, pushing on, whether followed or not.

And now the past few years comes a new thing. This surprising Jew is surprising us anew. From all corners of the earth they are gathering as not since the scattering to the Assyrian plains, gathering to discuss and plan for the getting into shape as a nation again on the old home soil. Jews of every sort, utterly diverse in every other imaginable way, except this of being Jews, men who hate each other intensely because of divergent beliefs in other matters, yet brushing elbows in annual gatherings to plan with all their old time intensity a new Jewish nation. Along the highways of earth, made and controlled by Christian peoples, they come. What does it mean? They continue to be, as they have been, the puzzle of history[15].

This tragic break of the kingdom and the persistency of the King's plan regardless of the break hold the key to the puzzle. The Jew has been preserved, divinely preserved, against every attempt at his destruction. For he is the keystone in the arch of the King's plan for a coming world-wide dominion.

Jesus is God's spirit-magnet for the Jew and for all men. Around Him they will yet gather, with the new Jewish nation in the lead, the church closest to the person of the king, and all men drawn. Jesus is God's organizer of the social fabric of the world. In response to His presence and touch, each in his own place will swing into line and make up a perfect social fabric.

With the new zeal for pure, holy living now in the church, the clearer vision coming to her of the Lord's purpose of evangelizing the world, the evidence in all parts of the world of men turning their thought anew to God, this remarkable Jewish movement toward national life, it is a time for earnest men to get off alone on bent knees, and with new, quietly deep fervour, to pray "Thy kingdom come." "Even so come, Lord Jesus."

---

[15] What is amazing about this passage is that this is written 1906! Nearly 50 years would pass before this became a fact and the new Nation of Israel would appear.

The person of Jesus

1. The Human Jesus.
2. The Divine Jesus.
3. The Winsome Jesus.

The Human Jesus

God's meaning of "human."

Jesus is God becoming man's fellow. He comes down by his side and says, "Let's pull up together." Jesus was a man. He was as truly human as though only human. We are apt to go at a thing from the outside. God always reaches within, and fastens His hook there. He finds the solution of every problem within itself. When He would lead man back the Eden road to the old trysting place under the tree of life He sent a man. Jesus takes His place as a man and refuses to be budged from the human level with His brothers.

That word human has come to have two meanings. The first true meaning, and a second, that has grown up through sin, and sin's taint and trail. The second has become the common popular meaning; the first, the forgotten meaning. It will help us live up to our true possible selves to mark keenly the distinction. The first is God's meaning, the true. The second is sin's, the hurt meaning. Constantly we read the effect and result of sin into God's thought as though that were the real thing. This is grained in deep, woven into the adages of the race. For instance, "To err is human, to forgive divine." Yet this catchy statement is not true, save in part. To forgive is human – God's human – as well as divine. Not to forgive is devilish. It is not human to err. It is possible to the human being to err, as it is with angels, but, in erring, man is leaving the human level and going lower down.

To understand what it means to say that Jesus is human we must recall what human meant originally, and has properly come to mean. Man as made by God before the hurt of sin came had certain powers and limitations. His powers, briefly, were, mastery of his body, of his mental faculties, and powers in the spirit realm so lost to us now that we cannot even say definitely what they are. And mastery means poised, mature control, not misuse, nor abuse, nor lack of use, but full proper use. Possibly there were powers of communication between men in addition to speech unknown to us. Then, too, he had dominion over nature, over all the animal creation, over all the forces of nature, and not only dominion, but fellowship with the animal creation and with the forces of nature: dominion through fellowship.

He had certain limitations. Having a body was a limitation. The necessity for food, sleep, rest, and for exertion in order to move through space acted as a constant check upon his movements and achievements. He could not go into a building except through some opening. The law of growth, of such infinite value to man under his conditions, was likewise a check. Only by slow laborious effort and application would there come the discipline of mental powers and the knowledge necessary to life's work.

The hurt of sin.

Now, in addition to these natural limitations sin has made other changes. It has lessened the powers and increased the limitations. There has been immense loss in the power over the forces of nature, though now, by slow and very laborious efforts, after centuries, much is being regained. Instead of fellowship there has been an estrangement between man and the lower animals and between man and the forces of nature. All of this has immensely added to man's limitations, though it is true that most men do not know of what has been lost, so complete has the loss been.

The natural limitations have been added to. Sin affects the judgment. It brings ignorance and passion, and they affect the judgment. There results lack of care of the body, improper use of the strength, and ignorant and improper use of the bodily functions. Then come weakness and disease and shortened life, not to speak of the misery included in these and the enjoyment missed. In the chain of results comes the toil that is drudgery. Not work, but excessive work, more than one should do, with less strength than one should have. Work itself under natural conditions is always a delight. But through sin has come strain, tugging, friction, unequal division. The changes wrought in nature by sin call for greater effort with less return. Toil becomes slavish and grinding. Then poverty adds its tug. And sorrow comes to sap the strength and take away the buoyancy. And then man's inhumanity to his brothers and sisters. These are some of the limitations added by sin and ever increasing.

Our fellow.

Now, Jesus was human; truly naturally human, God's human, and then more because of the conditions He found. The love act of creation brought with it self-imposed limitations to God. And now the love act of saving brings still more. God made man in His own image. In His humanity Jesus was in the image of God, even as we are. Adam was an unfallen man. Jesus was that and more, a tested and now matured unfallen man, and by the law of growth ever growing more. Adam was an innocent, unfallen man up to the temptation. Jesus was a virtuous unfallen man. The test with Him changed innocence to virtue.

In His experiences, His works, His temptations, His struggles, His victories, Jesus was clearly human. In His ability to read men's thoughts and know their lives without finding out by ordinary means, His knowledge ahead of coming events, His knowledge of and control over nature, He clearly was more than the human we know. Yet until we know more than we seem to now of the proper powers of an unfallen man matured and growing in the use and control of those powers we cannot draw here any line between human and divine. But the whole presumption is in favour of believing that in all of this Jesus was simply exercising the proper human powers which with Him were not hurt by sin but ever increasing in use.

Jesus insisted on living a simple true human life, dependent upon God and upon others. He struck the key-note of this at the start in the wilderness. Everything He taught He put through the test of use. He was what He taught. As a man He has gone through all He calls us to. He blazed the way into every thicket and woods, and then stands ahead, softly, clearly calling, "Come along after Me."

He was a normal man, God's pattern unchanged. All the powers of body and mind and spirit were developed naturally and held in poise, no lack of development, no over development of some part, no misuse of any power, nor abuse, but each part perfectly fitting in and working naturally with each other part.

He experienced all the proper limitations of human life. He needed food and sleep and rest and needed to give His body proper thought and care. He was under the human limitations regarding space and material construction. He got from one place to another by the slow process of using His strength or joining it with nature or that of a beast. He entered a building through an opening as we do. Both of these are in sharp contrast with the conditions after the resurrection. His stock of knowledge came by the law of increase, the natural way; some, and then more, and the more gaining more yet.

But there's more than this. There's a bit of a pull inside as one thinks of this, as though Jesus in His humanity after all is on a level above us, hardly alongside giving us a hand. Ah! there is more. He had fellowship with us in the limitation that sin has brought. He shared the experiences that men were actually having. He knew the bitterness of having one's life plan utterly broken and something else – a rude jagged something else – thrust in its place. But the bitterness of the experience never got into His spirit or affected His conduct. The emergency He found down here wrought by sin affected Him.

He was hungry sometimes without food at hand to satisfy His hunger. He always showed a peculiar tender sympathy with hungry people. He couldn't bear the sight of the hungry crowds without food. He would go out of His way any time to feed a man. He makes the caring for hungry folks a test question for the judgment time. There's a great note of sympathy here with the race. Every night hundreds of thousands of our brothers and sisters go hungry to bed. It was said at one time that the death rate of London rises and falls with the price of bread. If true when said it probably is more intensely true to-day. Jesus ate the bread of the poor, the coarsest, plainest bread. But then, that may have been simply His good common sense.

Jesus got tired. Could there be a closer touch! He fell asleep on a pillow in the stern of the boat one day crossing the lake. And the sleep was like that of a very tired man, so sound that the wild storm did not wake Him up. It was His tiredness that made Him wait at Jacob's well while the disciples push on to the village to get food. He wouldn't have asked them to go if they were too tired, too. Was He ever too tired – over-tired – like we get? I wonder. There was the temptation to be so ever tugging. Probably not, for He was wise, and had good self-control, and then He trusted His Father. Yet He probably went to the full limit of what was wise. Certainly He lived a strenuous life those three and a half years.

Jesus knew the pinch of poverty. He was the eldest in a large family, with the father probably dead, and so likely was the chief breadwinner, earning for Himself and for the others a living by His trade. He was the village carpenter up in Nazareth, an obscure country village. I do not mean abject grinding poverty, of course. That cannot exist with frugality and honest toil. But the pinch of constant management, rigid economy, counting the coins carefully, studying to make both ends meet, and needing to stretch a bit to get them together. It is not unlikely that house rent was one of the items.

The ceaselessness of His labours those public years suggests habits of industry acquired during those long Nazareth years. He was used to working hard and being kept busy. It would seem that He had the care of His mother after the home was broken up. At the very end He makes provision for her. John understands the allusion and takes her to his own home. He must have thought a great deal of John to trust His mother to his care. Could there be finer evidence of friendship than giving His friend John such a trust?

Jesus was a homeless man. Forced from the home village by His fellow townsmen, for those busy years he had no quiet home spot of His own to rest in. And He felt it. How He would have enjoyed a home of His own, with His mother in it with him! No more pathetic word comes from His lips than that touching His homelessness – foxes have holes, and the birds of the air nests, but the Son of Man hath neither hole nor nest, burrowed or built, in ground or tree.

And Jesus knew the sharp discipline of waiting. He knew what it meant to be going a commonplace, humdrum, tread-mill round while the fires are burning within for something else. He knew, and forever cast a sweet soft halo over all such labour as men call drudgery, which never was such to Him because of the fine spirit breathed into it. Drudgery, commonplaceness is in the spirit, not the work. Nothing could be commonplace or humdrum when done by One with such an uncommon spirit.

There's more of God since Jesus went back.

I have tried to think of Him coming into young manhood in that Nazareth home. He is twenty now, with a daily round something like this: up at dawn likely – He was ever an early riser – chores about the place, the cow, maybe, and the kindling and fuel for the day, helping to care for the younger children, then off down the narrow street, with a cheery word to passers-by, to the little low-ceilinged carpenter shop, for – eight hours? – more likely ten or twelve. Then back in the twilight; chores again, the evening meal, helping the children of the home in difficulties that have arisen to fill their day's small horizon, a bit of quiet talk with His mother about family matters, maybe, then likely off to the hilltop to look out at the stars and talk with the Father; then back again, slipping quietly into the bedroom, sharing sleeping space in the bed with a brother. And then the sweet rest of a labouring man until the grey dawn broke again.

And that not for one day, every day, a year of days – years. He's twenty-five now, feeling the thews[16] of his strength; twenty-seven, twenty-nine, still the old daily round. Did no temptation come those years to chafe a bit and fret and wonder and yearn after the great outside world? Who that knows such a life, and knows the tempter, thinks he missed those years, and their subtle opportunity? Who that knows Jesus thinks that He missed such an opportunity to hallow forever, fragrantly hallow, home, with its unceasing round of detail, and to cushion, too, its every detail with a sweet strong spirit? Who thinks He missed that chance of fellowship with the great crowd of His race of brothers?

"In the shop of Nazareth
Pungent cedar haunts the breath.
'Tis a low Eastern room,
Windowless, touched with gloom.
Workman's bench and simple tools
Line the walls. Chests and stools,
Yoke of ox, and shaft of plow,
Finished by the Carpenter
Lie about the pavement now.
"In the room the Craftsman stands,
Stands and reaches out His hands.
"Let the shadows veil His face
If you must, and dimly trace
His workman's tunic, girt with bands
At His waist. But His hands –
Let the light play on them;
Marks of toil lay on them.
Paint with passion and with care
Every old scar showing there
Where a tool slipped and hurt;
Show each callous; be alert
For each deep line of toil.
Show the soil

---

16 Thews – Muscles!

Of the pitch; and the strength
Grip of helve gives at length.
"When night comes, and I turn
From my shop where I earn
Daily bread, let me see
Those hard hands; know that He
Shared my lot, every bit:
Was a man, every whit.
"Could I fear such a hand
Stretched toward me? Misunderstand
Or mistrust? Doubt that He
Meets me full in sympathy?
"Carpenter' hard like Thine
Is this hand – this of mine;
I reach out, gripping Thee,
Son of Man, close to me,
Close and fast, fearlessly."[17]

To-day up yonder on the throne there's a Man – kin to us, bone of our bone, heart of our heart, toil of our toil. He – knows. If you'll listen very quietly, you'll hear His voice reaching clear down to you saying, with a softness that thrills, "Steady – steady – I know it all. I'm watching and feeling and helping. Up yonder is the hill top and the glory sun and the wondrous air. Steady a bit. Stay up with Me on the glory side of your cloud, though your feet scratch the clay." Surely there's more of God since Jesus went back!

The Divine Jesus

Jehovah – Jesus.

Of all the men who knew Jesus intimately John stands first and highest. He misunderstood for a time. He failed to understand, as did the others. He did not approach the keen insight into Jesus' being and purpose that Mary of Bethany did. But, then, she was a woman. He was a man. Other things being equal (though they almost never are), woman has keener insight into the spirit and motives than has man. But John stood

---

[17] Arthur P Vaughan

closer to Jesus than any other. Jesus drew him closer. And that speaks volumes for John's fineness of spirit. He alone of the inner twelve did not forsake in the hardest hour that Thursday night, but went in "with Jesus." How grateful must Jesus have been for the presence of His sympathetic friend that black night, with its long intense shadows!

Now John writes about Jesus. And what this closest friend says will be of intense interest to all lovers of Jesus. But it is of even more interest to note keenly when John writes. He waits until the end. He gets the longest range on Jesus that his lengthening years will permit. Distance is essential to perspective. You must get far away from a big thing to see it. The bigger the thing to be seen, the longer the distance needed for good perspective. John shows his early appreciation of the size of Jesus by waiting so long. When all his mental faculties are most matured, when any heat of mere youthful attachment has cooled off, when the eye of the spirit is clearest and keenest, when the facts through long sifting have fallen into right place and relation in the whole circle of truth, then the old man settles to his loving task.

He had been looking long. His perspective has steadily lengthened with the looking years. The object has been getting bigger and bigger to his eyes. He is getting off as far as possible within his earthly span. At last he feels that he has approximately gotten the range. And with the deep glow of his heart gleaming up out of his eyes, he picks up a freshly-sharpened quill to tell folk about Jesus.

As he starts in he takes a fresh, long, earnest look. And so he writes, like a portrait artist working, with his eyes ever gazing at the vision of that glorified Face. He seems to say to himself, "How shall I – how can I ever begin to tell them – about Him!" Then with a master's skill he sets out to find the simplest words he can find, put together in the simplest sentences he can make, so simple folk everywhere may read and get something of a glimpse of this Jesus, whose glory is filling his eyes and flooding his face and spilling out all over the pages as he writes.

He is seeing back so far that he is getting beyond human reach. So he fastens his line into the farthest of the far-reaches of human knowledge, the creation, and then flings the line a bit farther back yet. He must use a human word, if human folk are to understand. So he says "beginning." "In the beginning," the beginningless beginning, away back of the Genesis beginning, the earliest known to man.

Then he recalls the tremendous fact that when, in the later beginning man knew about, the worlds came into existence, it was by a word being spoken, a creative, outspoken word. The power that created things revealed itself in a few simple words. Then he searches into the depths of language for the richest word he knew to express thought outspoken. And taking that word he uses it as a name for this One of whom he is trying to tell. The scholars seem unable to sound the depths of the word that John in his own language uses. It means this, and beyond that, it means this, deeper yet, and then this. And then all of these together, and more. That is John's word. "In the beginning was the Word."

Then with a few swift touches of his pen he says, "This was Jesus before He came among men, the man Jesus whom we know." In the earliest beginning the whole heart and thought of God toward man was outspoken in a person. This person, this out speaking God, it was He who later became known to us as Jesus. Jesus, away back before the farthest reach of our human knowledge, was God speaking out of His inner heart to us. This Jesus is God speaking out His innermost heart to man. Did you ever long to hear God speak? Look at Jesus. He's God's speech. This One was with God. He was God. It was He who spoke things into being, that creative span of time. Only through Him could anything come into being. All life was in Him, and this life was man's light. It is He who came into our midst, shining in the darkness that could neither take Him in nor hold Him down from shining out.

Every now and then as he writes John's heart seems near the breaking point, and a sob shakes his pen a bit, as it comes over him all anew, and almost overcomes him, how this wondrous Jesus, this throbbing heart of God, was treated. Listen: "He came to His own possessions, and they who were His – own – kinsfolk – and the quiver of John's heart-sob seems to make the type move on the page – His own kinsfolk received him not into their homes, but left Him outside in the cold night; but – a glimpse of that glorious Face steadies him again – as many as did receive Him, whether His own kinsfolk or not, to them He gave the right to become kinsfolk of God, the oldest family of all."

God's spokesman.

John has a way of reaching away back, and then by a swift use of pen coming quickly to his own time, and then he keeps swinging back over the ground he has been over, but each time with some added touch, like the true artist he is.

John's statement, "the world was made by Him," takes one back at once to the early Genesis chapters. There the creating One, who, by a word, brings things into existence is called God. And then, that we may identify Him, is called by a name, Jehovah. The creator is God named Jehovah. And this Jehovah, John says, was the One who afterward became a Man, and pitched His tent among men. And as one reads the old chapters through, this is the God, the Jehovah, who appears in varying ways to these Old Testament men, one after another. He talked and walked and worked with Adam in completing the work of creation, and then broken-hearted led him out of the forfeited garden.

Then to make his standpoint unmistakably plain to everyone, before starting in on the witness borne by the herald, he makes a summary. All that he has been saying he now sums up in these tremendous words, "God – no one ever yet has seen; the only begotten God,7 in the bosom of the Father, this One has been the spokesman." In what He was, and in what He did as well as in what He said, He hath been the spokesman. Here is a difference made between the Father God, whom no one has seen, and the only begotten God, who has been telling the Father out.

Now God revealed Himself to men in the Old Testament times. Repeatedly in the Old Testament it distinctly speaks of men seeing God in varying ways and talking with Him. Adam walked with Him, and Enoch, and Noah. Abraham had a vision, and talked with the three men whose spokesman speaks as God. Isaac has a night-vision and Jacob a dream and a night meeting with a mysterious wrestler. Moses spoke with Him "face to face" and "mouth to mouth," and is said to have seen His "form." Yet after that first forty days on the mount when Moses hungrily asks for more, He is told that no man could endure the sight of that great glory of God's face. And he is put in to a cleft of the rock, and God's hand put over the opening (in the simple language of the record), and then only the hinder part of God passing is seen, while the wondrous voice speaks. Yet the impression so made upon Moses far exceeds anything previous and completely overawes and melts him down. The elders of Israel "saw God," yet the most distinct impression of anything seen is of the beautiful pavement under His feet. Isaiah's most definite impression, when the great vision came to him, was of a train of glory, seraphim and smoke and a voice. Ezekiel has rare power in detailed description. He has overpowering visions of the "glory of Jehovah." Yet the most definite that he can make the description is a storm gathering, a cloud, a fire, a centre spot of brightness, a clearness as of amber, and four very unusual living creatures.

These men "saw" God. He "appeared" to them. Evidently that means many different things, yet the word is always honestly used. It never means as we gaze into another man's face. But always there is that profound impression of having been in God's own presence. They met Him. They saw Him. They heard His voice.

Yet John says here, "God – no one ever yet at any time has seen; the only begotten God, in the bosom of the Father – this One has been the spokesman." Clearly John, sweeping the whole range of past time, means this: they saw Him whom we call Jesus. Jesus is Jehovah, the only begotten God. To all these men the only begotten God was the spokesman of the Father.

Sometimes it was a voice that came with softness but unmistakable clearness to the inner spirit of man, a soundless voice. Sometimes in a dream, a more realistic vision of the night or of the day time; again, in the form of a man, thus foreshadowing the future great coming. This One who came to them in various ways, this Jehovah has come to men as Jesus. This is John's statement. This is the setting of His gospel. The setting becomes a part of the interpretation of what the gospel contains. It explains what this that follows meant to John.

Is it surprising that John's Gospel has been pitched upon as the critics' chief battlefield of the New Testament? Battlefield is a good word. The fire has been thick and fast, needle-guns – sharp needles – and machine-guns – Gatling guns and rattling – but no smokeless powder. The cloud of smoke of a beautiful scholarly grey tinge has quite filled the air. Men have been swinging away from a man, the Man to a book. But no critic's delicately shaded and shadowing cloud of either dust or smoke, or both, can hide away the Man. He's too tall and big. The simple hearted man who will step aside from the smoke and noise to the shade of a quiet tree, or the quiet of some corner, with this marvellous bit of manuscript from John's pen for his keen, Spirit-cleared eye, will be enraptured to find a Man, the Man, the God-Man.

Whom Moses saw.

What did Jesus say about Himself? The critics of the world, including the sceptical, infidel critics, seem to agree fully and easily on a few things about this Jesus on whose dissection they have expended so much time and strength. They agree that in the purity of His life, the moral power of His character, the wisdom of His teachings, the rare poise of His conduct and judgment, the influence exerted upon men, He clear over-tops the whole race. Surely His own opinion of Himself is well worth having. And it is easy to get, and tremendous when gotten. It fits into John's conception with unlaboured simplicity and naturalness.

According, then, to Jesus' own words, He had come down out of heaven, and, by and by, would go back again to where He was before. He had come on an errand for the Father down into the world, and when the errand was finished He would go back home to the Father again. He had seen the Father, and He was the only one who had ever seen Him. He was the Son of God in a sense that nobody else was, a begotten Son, and the only Son who had been begotten. Therefore, He naturally called God His Father, and not only that, but His Own Father, making Himself equal with the Father.

This statement it was that swung the leaders over from silent contempt to aggression in their treatment of Him. The Jews understood this perfectly and instantly. They refused to accept it. Reckoning it blasphemous, they attempted to stone Him. They were partly right. If it were not true, it was blasphemous, and their law required stoning. Yet they were fools in their thought, and not even keen fools. For no blasphemous man could have revealed the character and moral glory that Jesus constantly revealed before their eyes.

Then follows one of John's exquisite reports of Jesus' words in reply. In it run side by side the essential unity of spirit between Father and Son, with the absolute life-giving or creative power invested in the Son. A sweet, loving, loyal unity of spirit is between the two. It is love unity. There can be none closer. In this unity the Son has full control of life for all the race of men, and final adjustment of the character wrought out by each. At His word all who have gone down under death's touch will come into life again, and each by the character he has developed will go by a moral gravitation to his natural place.

And then follows the bringing forward of witnesses, John, the Father, the works, the Scriptures, and the climax is reached in the one whose name was ever on their lips – Moses. And this is the significant reference to Moses, "He wrote of Me." Sift into that phrase a bit. It cannot mean, he wrote of me in the sacrifices provided for with such minute care. For Moses clearly had had no such thought. It might be supposed to mean that unconsciously to himself there was, in his writings about the sacrifices, that which would be seen later to refer to Jesus in His dying. And there is the resemblance in purity between Moses' sacrifices and the great Sacrifice. Yet where there is so much plain meaning lying out on the face of the thing, this obscure meaning may be dropped or checked in as an incidental. There is a single allusion in Moses' writing to a prophet coming like himself.

But Moses is ever absorbed in writing about a wondrous One who revealed Himself to him in the burning bush, the pillar of cloud and fire, the little peaked tent off by itself on the outskirts of the camp, and the soft distinct voice. There was the One with whom He had twice spent forty days in the mount, and whose great glory left its traces in his face. Ever Moses is writing of this wondrous Jehovah. Jesus quietly says, "He wrote of Me."

Another time He said, "I and the Father are one," provoking another stoning. Invisibly holding back their hands He said, "The Father is in Me, and I in the Father," and again they are aroused. In connection with this word "Father," it may be noted that the Old Testament has been called the "dispensation of the Father." But this seems scarcely accurate. God speaking, appearing there is spoken of as Father very rarely, and then chiefly in the great promises of the future glory. The common name for Him is Jehovah. Jesus practically gives us the name Father for God. He constantly refers to God as His Father. It was He who taught us to call God Father. He never speaks of Jehovah, but of the Father. His language in this always fits in perfectly, as of course it would, with John's standpoint, that Jesus is the Jehovah of the Old Testament times. A little later Jesus says, "Moses gave you not the manna from heaven, but – my Father giveth (note the change in the time element of the word) – giveth you the true bread." It is a sort of broken, readjusted sentence, as though He was going to say who it was that gave the manna, and then changes to speaking of the Father and the present. He does not say who it was that did give that manna. It is plain enough from John's standpoint what he understands Jesus to mean as he puts the incident into his story.

Jesus is God wooing man.

During the autumn before His death, while in attendance on one of the Jerusalem feasts, the leaders are boasting of their direct descent from Abraham, and attacking Jesus. On their part the quarrel of words gets very bitter. They ask sharply, "Who do you pretend to be? Nobody can be as great as Abraham; yet your words suggest that you think you are." Then came from Jesus' lips the words, spoken in all probability very quietly, "Your father Abraham exulted that he might see my day, and he saw it, and was glad." It is a tremendous statement, staggering to one who has not yet grasped it.

In attempting to find its meaning, some of our writing friends have supposed it means that, after Abraham's death, when he was in the other world, at the time of Jesus being on the earth, he was conscious of Jesus having come and was glad. But this hardly seems likely, else it would read, "He sees, and is glad." The seeing and gladness were both in a day gone by. Others have supposed that it refers to the scene on Moriah's top, when the ram used as a sacrifice instead of Isaac enabled Abraham to see ahead by faith, not actually, the coming One. But this, too, seems a bit far-fetched, because Abraham was surprised by the occurrences of that day. He fully expected to sacrifice his son, apparently, so there could be no exultant looking forward to that day for him. And deeper yet, the coming One was not expected to be a sacrifice, but a king.

The natural meaning seems to lie back in Abraham's own life. Abraham was Israel's link with the idolatrous heathen, as well as the beginning of the new life away from idolatry. He grew up among an idolatrous people, yet in his heart there was a yearning for the true God. Back in his old home there came to him one day the definite inner voice to cut loose from these people, his own dear kinsfolk, and go out to a strange unknown land, with what seemed an indefinite goal, and there would come to him a vision of the true God.

It was a radical step for a man of seventy-five years to take. He was living among his own kinsfolk. His nest was feathered. It meant leaving a certainty for an uncertainty. It meant breaking his habit of life, a very hard thing to do, and starting out on a wandering roaming life. Not unlikely his neighbours thought it a queer thing, a wild goose chase, this going off to a strange land in response to a call of God that he might see a vision of the true God. Decidedly visionary. But the old man was clear about the voice. The fire burned within to know God, the real true God. All else counted as nothing against that. He would see God. And a warming glow filled his heart and shone in his eyes and kept him steady during the break, the good-byes, the start away, the journeying among strangers. Into the strange land he came, and pitched his tent. And – one night – in his tent – among these strange Canaanites, there came the promised vision. "Jehovah appeared unto Abraham," and tied up there anew with him the promise made back in his native land. This seems to be the simple explanation of these words about Abraham. "He exulted that he might see my day. He saw ... and was glad."

With a contemptuous curl of the lip instantly they come back with: "Thou art not yet fifty years old, and hast thou seen Abraham?" More quietly than ever, with the calmness of conscious truth, come those tremendous words, emphasized with the strongest phrase He ever used, "Verily, verily, I say unto you, before Abraham was born, I am." The common version omits "born," and so the sharp contrast is not made clear. Abraham was born. He came into existence. Jesus says "I am." That "I am" is meant to mean absolute existence. An eternal now without beginning or ending. Their Jewish ears are instantly caught by that short sentence. Jesus was identifying Himself with the One who uttered that sentence out of the burning bush! Again stones for speech. Again the invisible power holds their feverish impotent hands. That "I am" explains the meaning of the expression "my day." It stretches it out backward beyond Abraham's day. It lengthens it infinitely at both ends.

This is Jesus' point of view, this marvellous Jesus. He is the Jehovah in Genesis' first chapters. It is with Him that Adam broke tryst that day, and with Him that Enoch renewed the tryst after such a long wait, and took those long walks. It is His voice and presence in the black topped, flaming mount that awed the Israel crowd so. His voice it was that won and impressed so winsomely the man waiting in the hand-covered cleft of the rock that early morning, and long after, that other rugged, footsore man, standing with face covered in the mouth of a cave. Isaiah saw His glory that memorable day in the temple. It was He who rode upon the storm before Ezekiel's wondering eyes and who walks with His faithful ones on the seven times heated coals, and reveals to Daniel's opened ears the vision of his people's future. Jehovah – He comes as Jesus. Jesus – He is Jehovah. No sending of messengers for this great work of winning His darling back to the original image and mastery and dominion will do for our God. He comes Himself. Jesus is God coming down to woo man up to Himself again.

The Winsome Jesus

The face of Jesus

Jesus was God letting man see the beauty of His face and listen to the music of His voice, and feel the irresistibly gentle drawing power of His presence. Jesus was very winsome. He drew men. He said that if He were lifted up He would draw men. They who heard that could believe it, for He drew them before He was lifted up. He drew the crowds. Yet many a leader that has drawn the crowds has led them astray. He drew men – men of strongest mentality, scholarly, cultured, thoughtful men, and every other sort. Yet men have often been befooled in their leaders. He drew women. Here is a great test. Men may be deceived in a man. But woman, true strong woman, pure womanly woman, because of her keen discernment into spirit and motive, cannot be deceived, when true to her inner conviction.

He drew children. This was the highest test. The child, fresh from the hand of God, before it is appreciably hurt by parents or surroundings, is drawn to the pure and good. They are repelled by selfishness and badness. They draw out the best. They are drawn only by the true and beautiful and good. That is, in the early years, before the warping of a selfish, sinful atmosphere has hurt them. This is an infallible test. This told most His winsomeness.

Bad people were drawn to Him. That is, bad in their lives. Rarely indeed is a human so wholly bad as to be untouched by true goodness, by sincere love. Here is the touchstone of service. He touched that spot in the lowest, and by His presence increased the hunger of their hearts for purity and for sympathy up toward purity.

His enemies – a very small group, but in a position of great power, holding the national reins – His enemies were drawn to Him, by a drawing they fought, but could not resist. They admired Him while hating Him. His presence disturbed because it accused the opposite in them. They recognized the purity, the love, the rugged honesty, the keen insight, the poised wisdom, and they hated Him the more intensely, so committed were they in the practice of their lives to the opposite of these. Jesus was very winsome. It was to be expected of Him, for He was a man unstained and unhurt by sin. Man, God's sort of man, is winsome, for he is in the image of God. It was to be expected of Him, for He was God. And God is winsome. Did men but know God they would throw themselves at His feet in the utter abandon of strong love.

Jesus' personality must have been very attractive, because of the man living within. He found expression in it. The spirit of a man finds expression in his presence. He goes out to others through his presence. From what we know of Jesus His presence must have had something distinctly impressive about it. He would have a gently majestic bearing. He walked upright like the king He was. He had the true dignity that is not conscious of its dignity.

Jesus must have had a remarkable face. One's presence centres peculiarly in the face. It comes to bear the imprint of the man inside. A man cannot keep out of his face the dominant spirit of his life. The sin of the life, the purity of the heart, is always stamped on the face. The finer the nature the plainer is the facial index. That is the reason women's faces reveal the inner spirit more than men's. Quite apart from His features, the inner spirit of Jesus must have made His face beautiful with a manly fascinating beauty. Yet in all likelihood those features were finely chiselled and the skin clear, and with the transfiguring power of the spirit within, that face must have been a great face in its beauty.

Jesus' face must have borne the impress of His experiences. The early home experience would bring out patience and simplicity and sympathy. Those forty days in the wilderness would intensify the purity and strength, and bring evidence of struggle and of victory. The Jordan waters, with the voice of approval, would deepen the mark of peace. Constant contact with the sick and suffering would bring out yet more the tenderness and gentleness. Constant teaching of undisciplined folk would intensify the patience. Constant contact with sin would intensify the unflinching sternness of purity. The Transfiguration would deepen the spirituality, with possibly an added glory-touch. Gethsemane wrote in the deep lines of intense suffering, with the intangible spirituality of victory and great peace. And, at the last, Calvary with its scars marked in a beauty of suffering and of spirituality refined beyond description. A marvellous face that human face of Jesus.

Indeed, the glory of God was in the face of Jesus as He walked quietly among men. Looking into that face men saw God. That simple, gentle, patient, pure face, with its deep peace and victory and yet its yearning – that was God looking out into men's faces.

The music of God in the voice of Jesus.

The face of that face was the eye. The eye is the soul of the face. Through it the man looks out and shows himself. Through it we look in and see him. Where the fires of self-ambition burn the flame is always in the eye. Only where those fires are out or never lit does the real beauty-light of God come into the eye. Great leaders have ever been noted for their eyes, before whose glance strong men have cowed and quailed, or eagerly coveted the privilege of service.

Those must have been matchless eyes of Jesus, keen, kindly, flashing out blinding lightning, sending out softest subdued light. The Nazareth mob couldn't stand the look of those eyes, nor the bolder Jerusalem mob reaching down for the stones, nor the deputation sent to arrest, nor even the reckless Roman soldiers at the garden gate. The disciples who were closest sometimes followed him afraid and amazed because of the look of those eyes. And yet the little children put their arms around His neck, and looked up fearlessly and lovingly. And the crowd listened by the hour with their eyes fastened upon His.

The voice of Jesus must have been music itself. It speaks once of His singing a hymn. How we would all have loved to hear Him sing! But that voice was music at all times, whether in song or speech. Low, modulated, rhythmic, gentle, rich, resonant – wondrous music. Those who have heard Spurgeon and Gladstone almost always speak of the rare musical quality in their voices. So, and more would it be with this Jesus. It has been said that the personality reveals itself in the speech. It reveals itself yet more, and more subtly, in the sound of the voice. The power or weakness of a man is felt in the sound of his voice. The blind have unusual skill in reading character in the voice. Were we wiser we could read men's character much more quickly in the voice. Children and animals do. The voice that stilled the waves and spoke forgiveness of sins, that drew the babes, and talked out to thousands at once, must have been full of sweetest music and thrilling with richest power.

Jesus made much of the personal touch, another means whereby a man's power goes out to his fellow. He believed in close personal touch. He drew men into close contact with Himself. He promised that when gone Himself, somebody else was to come, and live as He had done right with us in close touch. He touched those whom He helped, regardless of conditions. There was power in His touch. Some of Himself went out through that touch of His. The fever, the weakness, the disease fled before His touch.

Is it to be wondered at that everywhere, in the temple yards, on Judean hills or Galilean, by the blue waters of Galilee or the brown waters of the Jordan, men crowded to Jesus? They couldn't help it. He was irresistible in His presence, His face, His eye, and voice and touch. It could not be otherwise. He was God on a wooing errand after man. Moses' request of Jehovah, "Show me ... Thy glory," was being granted now to the whole nation. In Jesus they were gazing on the glory of God. A veiled glory? Yes, much veiled, doubtless, yet not as much as when Moses looked and listened.

Jesus draws men. All classes, all nations, all peoples are drawn to Him. It is remarkable how all classes in Christendom quote Jesus, and claim Him as the leader of their own particular views. They will selfishly claim Him who will not follow Him.

Jesus draws us. Let us each yield to His drawing. That is the sincerest homage and honour we can give Him. That will draw out in us to fullest measure the original God-likeness obscured by sin.

Let us lift this drawing Jesus up by our lives of loyalty to Him, by our modest, earnest testimony for Him, by our unselfish love for the men He loved so. Up let us lift Him before men's eyes; up on the cross, transfigured by His love; up on the Olives' Mount, Victor over all the forces of sin and death; up at the Father's right hand in glory, waiting the fullness of time for the completion of His plan for man.

Thou great winsome God, we have seen Thy beauty in this Jesus. We have heard Thy music in His voice. We feel the strong pull upon our hearts and wills of Thy presence in Him. We cannot resist Thee if we would. We would not if we could. We are coming a-running to keep tryst with Thee under the tree of life thou art planting down in our midst. We will throw ourselves at Thy feet in the utter abandon of our strongest love, Thy volunteer slaves.

The great experiences of Jesus' life

The Jordan: The Decisive Start

The anvil of experience.

Experience is going through a thing yourself, and having it go through you. And "through" here means not as a spear is thrust through a man's body, piercing it, but as fire goes through that which it takes hold of, permeating; as an odour goes through a house, pervading it.

A man knows only what he experiences; what he goes through; what goes through him. He knows only what he is certain of. And he is certain of only that which he experiences.

It is one of the natural limitations of our humanity that it is so. Even the primary knowledge of space, and time, and so on comes in this way. A man knows space only by seeing or thinking through space. He knows time only by living consciously through some moments of time. Such knowledge is primary only in point of time.

Experience is weaving fact into the fabric of your life. The swift drive of the double-pointed shuttle, the hard push of the loom back and forth goes through you.

Experience is sowing truth in actual personal occurrences. The cutting, upturning edge of the plough, the tearing teeth of the harrow[18], go on inside your very being, while perhaps the moments drag themselves by, slow as snails.

Experience is hammering truth into shape upon the anvil of your life, while the pounding of the lightning trip-hammer is upon your own

---

[18] an implement consisting of a heavy frame set with teeth or tines that is dragged over plowed land to break up clods, remove weeds, and cover seed.

quivering flesh. It is seeing that which is most precious to you, so dear as to be your very life, seeing that in a furnace, seven times heated, while you, standing helplessly by, hope and trust perhaps, and yet wonder, even while trusting, wonder if – (shall I say it the way your heart talks it out within?), or, at most, wonderingly watch with heart almost stopped, and eyes big, to see if the form of the fourth will intervene in your case, or whether something else is the Father's will.

Experience is the three young Hebrews stepping with quiet, full, heel-to-toe tread into the hotly flaming furnace, not sure but it meant torture and death, only sure that it was the only right thing to do. It is the old Babylonian premier actually lowering nearer and nearer to those green eyes, and yawning jaws, and ivories polished on many a bone, clear of duty though not clear of anything else.

A man having a financial understanding with his church, or a contract with his employer, or a comfortable business, may be an earnest Christian, living a life of prayer and realizing God's power in his life, but he cannot know the meaning of the word trust as George Mueller knew it when he might waken in the morning with not enough food in hand for the breakfast, only an hour off, of the two thousand orphans under his care, and in answer to his waiting prayer have them all satisfied at the usual breakfast hour. George Mueller himself did not know the meaning of "trust" before such experiences as he did afterwards. No one can. We know only what we experience.

Now Jesus became a perfect man by means of the experiences He went through. He is an older Brother to us, for He has gone through ahead where we are now going, and where we are yet to go. He was perfectly human in this, that He did not know our human experiences, save as He Himself went through those experiences. With full reverence be it said of the divine Jesus, it was necessarily so, because He was so truly human.

The whole diapason[19] of human experience, with its joyous majors and its sobbing minors, He knew. Except, of course, the experiences growing out of sin. These He could not know. They belong to the abnormal side of life. And there was nothing abnormal about Him. It was fitting that Jesus, coming as a man to save brother men, should develop the full human character through experience. And so He did. And forever He

[19] Diapason – a tonal grouping of the flue pipes of a pipe organ – probably meant to represent "full range of"

has a fellow-feeling with each of us, at every point, for He Himself has felt our feelings.

Jesus' experiences brought Him suffering; keen, cutting pain; real suffering. Where there is possible danger or pain in an approaching experience there is shrinking. It is a normal human trait to shrink from pain and danger. Jesus' experiences in the suffering they brought to Him far outreach what any other human has known. He shrank in spirit over and over again as the expected experiences approached. He shrank back as none other ever has, for He was more keenly alive to the suffering involved. He suffered doubly: in the shrinking beforehand; in the actual experience.

But, be it keenly remembered, shrinking does not mean faltering. Neither suffering in anticipation nor actually ever held Him back for a moment, nor an inch's length, nor in the spirit of full-tilted obedience to His Father's plan. This makes Jesus' experiences the greatest revelations of His character. He was sublime in His character, His teachings, His stupendous conceptions. He was most sublime in that wherein He touches us most closely – His experiences.

With a new, deep meaning it can be said, knowledge is power. We humans enter into knowledge and so into power only through experience. Experiences are sent, or when not directly sent are allowed to come, that through these may come knowledge, through knowledge power, through both the likeness of God, and so, true service in helping men back to God.

Let us, you and I, go through our experiences graciously, not grudgingly, not balking, cheerily, aye, with a bit of joy in the voice and a gleam of light in the eye. And remember, and not forget, that alongside is One who knows the experience that just now is ours, and, knowing, sympathizes.

There were with Jesus the commoner experiences and the great outstanding ones: the mountain range with the foot-hills below and the towering peaks above. From His earliest consciousness until the cross was reached, Jesus ran the whole gamut of human experiences common to us all, with some greater ones, which are the same as come to all men, but with Him intensified clear beyond our measurements.

These greater experiences were tragic until the great tragedy was past. Each has in it the shadow of the greatest. The Jordan waters meant turning from a kingdom down another path to a cross. The Wilderness fight pointed clearly to successive struggles, and the greatest. The Transfiguration mount meant turning from the greatest glory of His divinity which any earthly eye had seen to the little hill of death, which was to loom above the mount. Gethsemane is Calvary in anticipation. Calvary was the tragedy when love yielded to hate and, yielding, conquered. There love held hate's climax, death, by the throat, extracted the sting, drew the fang tooth, and drained the poison sac underneath. Love's surgery.

And the tinge of the tragedy remains in the Resurrection and Ascension in lingering scars. They are still in that face. It is a scale ascending from the first. In each is seen the one thing from a different angle. The cross in advance is in each experience, growing in intensity till itself is reached, and casting its shadow as it is left behind.

Our brother.

Through the crowds at the Jordan River, there quietly walked one morning a Man who came up to where John stood. He took a place in the line of those waiting to be baptized, so indicating His own intention. John is absorbed in his work, but as he faces this Man, next in order, he is startled. This is no ordinary man. That face! Its wondrous purity! That intangible something revealing the man! That spirit looking through those eyes into his own! In that presence he feels his own impurity. It is the instant unpremeditated recognition by this fine-grained Spirit-taught John of his Master, his Chief. The remonstrance that instinctively springs to his lips is held in check by the obedience he at once feels is due this One. Whatever He commands is right, however unexpected it may be, or however strange it may seem.

Why did Jesus go to John for baptism? The rite was a purifying one. It meant confession of sin, need of cleansing, a desire for cleansing, a purpose to turn from wrong and sin and lead a new life. How could Jesus accept such a rite for Himself? Why did He? Read in the light of the whole story of Jesus the answer seems simple. Jesus was stepping down into the ranks of man as His Brother. The kingdom He was to establish among men was to be set up and ruled over by man's Brother. The salvation was to be by One, close up, alongside. The King will brush elbows with His subjects, for they are brothers too. No long-range work for Jesus, but personal touch.

In accepting John's baptism, Jesus was allying Himself with the race of men He had come to lead up, and out, as King. He was allying Himself with them where they were. It was not the path always trodden by man in climbing to a throne. But it was the true path of fellowship with them in their needs. He was getting hold of hands, that He might be their leader up to the highlands of a new life. He steps to their level. He would lift from below. He would get by the side of the man lowest down. It was clear evidence at the start that He was the true Messiah, the King. He was their Brother. He would get down alongside, and pull up with them side by side out of the ditch of sticky mud up to good footing.

And mark keenly – and the heart glows a bit at the thought – the point He chooses for getting into that contact with His brothers. It is the point where they are turning from sin. John's baptism meant turning from sin. It is at that point that Jesus comes forward. A man can always be live-sure of Jesus meeting him there, close up, with outstretched hand. He is waiting eagerly, and steps up quickly to a man's side as in his heart he turns from sin.

But there's more yet. Read in the after light cast upon it there is much more. This was the voluntary path away from the kingdom. It was the beginning of all that came after. The road up the hill of the cross not far away led out of those waters. This was the starting point. Jesus calmly turned His face for the time being – a long time it has proved – away from the promised Kingdom of His Father and toward the planned cross of Satan.

It meant much, for it was the first step into the path marked out. What the Father had chosen for Him, He now chooses out for Himself. So every bit of service, every plan, must be twice chosen: by God for a man; by the man for himself as from God. He entered eagerly, for this was His Father's plan. That itself was enough for Jesus. But, too, it was the path where His needy brothers were. That would quicken His pace. It was the road wherein He would meet the enemy. And with a fresh prayer in His heart and a quiet confidence in His eye He steps into the road with that calmness that strong purpose gives.

As it proved there was danger here for Him. This was not the way approved by man's established ideals for starting a kingdom. He was driving straight across the carefully marked out roads of man's usage. He was disregarding the "No trespassing" signs. There was danger here. A man cutting a new path right across old ones meets stubborn undergrowth, and ugly thorn hedges. Jesus struck the thorns early, and right along to the last getting sharper. And they tore His face badly, as He cut the way through for His brothers.

Yes, there were dangers as He pushed His way through the undergrowth down to the water. Poison ivy thick, and fanged snakes darting guiltily aside from fear even while wanting to strike in, tangled, gnarly roots hugging the ground close, and bad odours and gases, and the light obscured – dangers thick! And these Jordan waters prove chill and roily. His stepping in stirs the mud. The storm winds sweep down the valley. A bit of a hill up above to the west casts a long sinister shadow out over the water.

And He must have known the dangers. No need of supernatural knowledge here. His familiarity with David and Jeremiah and other Hebrew writers, His knowledge of human nature as it had grown to be, His knowledge of a foe subtler than human, the fine sensitiveness of His finely organized sensitive spirit – these would lead Him to scent the danger.

But He falters not. The calmness of His will gives steadiness to His step down the river's bank. Aye, the dangers lured Him on. He had a keen scent for danger, for it was danger to His race of men, whose King He was in right and would prove Himself in fact. He would draw the thorn points by His own flesh that men might be saved their stinging prod and slash. He would neutralize the burning acid poison of the undergrowth by the red alkaline from His own veins. He would use the thorns to draw the healing salve for the wounds they had caused. He would put His firm foot on the serpent's head that His brothers might safely come along after. This was the meaning of His plunge into the swift waters by John's side.

The intense significance of this decisive step by Jesus is brought out strikingly by what follows. What followed is God's comment upon it. Quick as the act was done came the Father's approval. John's crowds were not the only intent lookers-on that day. Jesus stands praying. Since He is going this road it must be a-knee. Then the rift in the upper blue, the Holy Spirit straight from the Father's presence comes upon the waiting Man and the voice of pleased approval. And the heart of Jesus thrilled with the sound of that approving voice. He could go any length, down any steep, if He might only ever hear that voice in approval. Then the Holy Spirit took possession of Him for the earth-mission. In the pathway of obedience down that rough steep came the coveted power of God upon Him.

Three times in His life the Father's voice came, and each time at a crisis. Now at the plunge into the Jordan waters, which meant brotherhood with the race, and meant, too, a frostier chill of other waters later on. At

112

the opening of the Greek door through which led an easy path to a great following, and away from a cross, when Jesus, with an agony intensified by the intensified nearing of those crossed logs, turned His step yet more steadily in the path He had chosen that first Jordan day. And between these two, on the mountain top, when the whole fabric of the future beyond the cross hung upon three poor wobbling, spiritually stupid, mentally untrained Galilean fishermen.

This is the meaning of that step into the Jordan. It was the decisive start.

The Wilderness: Temptation

The University of Arabia.

The Jordan led to the Wilderness by a straight road. A first step without slipping leads to the second. Victory opens the way to fresh struggles for higher victories. The perfect naturalness of Jesus is revealed here, His human naturalness. He had taken the decisive step into the Jordan waters. And while absorbed in prayer had become conscious of a new experience. The Spirit of God came upon Him in unusual measure. The effect of that always is to awaken to new alertness and vigour every mental power, as well as to key up every moral resolve. Jesus is caught at once by the grasp, the grip of this new experience of the wondrous Spirit's control. Keenly alive to its significance, awakened anew to the part He was to perform, and to a consciousness of His peculiar relation to God and to man, He becomes wholly absorbed in this newly intensified world of thought.

Under the Spirit's impulse, He goes off into the solitude of the wilderness to think. And in this mood of deep absorption, with every faculty fully awake and every high moral impulse and purpose in full throb, came the temptation with the recorded climax at the close.

There came an intensifying of all His former consciousness, and convictions, regarding His own personality and His mission to mankind, as absorbed from the Hebrew parchments, with the undercurrent, lying away down, of a tragedy to be met on the way up to the throne.

Jesus was a man of great intensity. He could become so absorbed as to be unconscious of other things. As a boy of twelve, when first He caught fire, He was so taken up with the flood of thoughts poured into His mind by the temple visit, that for three days and two nights He remained away from His parents, simply absorbed in the world of thought awakened by that visit. He could remain forty days in the wilderness without being conscious of hunger. The impress of that forty days mentally remain with Him during the remainder of His human life. Intensity is possible only to strong mentality. The child's mind, the undisciplined mind, the mind weakened by sickness or fatigue goes quickly from one thing to another. The finest mental discipline is revealed in the greatest intensity, while yet all the faculties remain at normal, not heated, nor disturbed by the discoloration of heat.

He withdrew into the wilderness to think and pray. He wanted to get away from man that He might realize God. With the near flaming footlights shut out, He could see clearly the quiet upper lights, His sure guides. These forty days gave Him the true perspective. Things worked into proportion. He never lost this wilderness perspective. The wilderness means to Him alone with God, the false perspective, the flaming of near lights, the noise of men's shuffling feet all gone. And when He went out among men for work, that wilderness atmosphere went with Him. And when the crowds thickened, and work piled up, and dangers intensified, off He would go for a fresh bit of improvised wilderness.

The temptation follows the natural lines of man's powers. Man was made with mastery of himself, kingship over nature and all its forces, and utter dependence, even for his very breath, upon God. While made perfect in these, he would know them fully only through growth. He had three relationships, to God, his fellows, and himself. His relation to God would keep true the relation to himself, and adjust the relation to his fellows. Keeping God in proper proportion in the perspective keeps one's self in its true place always. Utter dependence by every man upon God would make perfect harmony with his fellows. The dominion of nature was through self-mastery, and this in turn would be only through the practice of utter dependence upon God.

Now all sin comes under this grouping, the relation to God, the relation to others, within one's self. Temptation follows the line of exaggeration, misuse, maladjustment, wrong motive. It pushes trust over into unwarranted presumption. Dominion over nature crosses the line into the relation to other men. Fellow-feeling gives way to an ambition to get ahead of the other man and to boss him. Proper appetite and desire become lust and passion. The dominion that man was to have over nature, he seeks also to have over his brothers, so crossing the line of his own proper dominion and trespassing on God's. Only God is to have dominion over all men. Where a man is lifted to eminence of rule among his fellows he is simply acting for Somebody else. He is not a superior. He is a servant of God, in ruling over his fellows.

John's famous grouping of all sin as "the lust of the flesh, lust of eye and pride of life," refers to what is out "in the world." It touches only two of these three: sin in one's self and in relation to his fellows, with the dominion line out of adjustment. Out in the world God has been left clean out, so the phase of trust isn't touched upon by John.

Jesus' temptation follows these natural lines. Improper use of power for the sake of the bodily appetite; to presume on God's care in doing something unwarranted; to cross the line of dominion over nature and seek to control men. For, be it remembered, Jesus was here as a man. The realm of the body, the realm of religion, the realm of wrong ambition, these were the temptation lines followed then, and before, and ever since.

The going into the wilderness was planned by the Holy Spirit. He was in charge of this campaign of Jesus to win back the allegiance of man and the dominion of the earth. Jesus yielded Himself to the control of the Holy Spirit for His earthly mission, even as later the Holy Spirit yielded Himself wholly to the control of the exalted Jesus for His earthly mission.

Here the Spirit proves Himself a keen strategist. He drives hard at the enemy. He forces the fighting. A decided victory over the chief at the start would demoralize all the forces. It would be decisive of the whole conflict, and prophetic of the final outcome. Every demon possessing a man on the earth heard of his chief's rout that day, and recognized his Victor, and feared Him, and knew of his own utter defeat in that of his chief. Having gotten the chief devil on the run, every sub-devil fled at Jesus' approach.

The Spirit would show to man the weakness of the devil. The devil can do nothing with the man who is calmly set in his loyalty to God. This new Leader of the race was led up to the dreaded devil that men might know for all time his weak spot. The poison of those fangs is completely neutralized by simple, steady loyalty to God. But the rattles do make a big scary noise.

It is safe to go where the Spirit of God leads, and not safe to go anywhere else. The wilderness, any wilderness, becomes a place of victory if the Spirit of God be leading there. Any temptation is a chance for a victory when the Spirit leads the way. A man's controlling motive determines the attractiveness or ugliness of any place. To Jesus this wilderness barren was one of the mountain peaks. Its forbidding chasms and ugly gullies and darting snakes ever afterwards speak to Him of sweet victory. The first great victory was here. He made the wilderness to blossom with the rose of His unswerving loyalty to His Father. And its fragrance has been felt by all who have followed Him there. To the tempter it was a wilderness indeed, barren of anything he wanted. He quit it the first chance he could make. He would remember the beasts and serpents and dreary waste. For here he received his first death-thrust.

Every man whom God has used has been in the wilderness. The two great leaders before Jesus, and the great leader after Him, had each a post-graduate course in the University of Arabia. A degree in that school is required for those who would do valiant service for God. Only so can the eyes and ears be trained away from the glare and blare of the crowd. They needed it, we need it, for discipline. He, the matchless Man, for that too, and that He might make it a place of sure victory for us.

Earth's ugliest, deepest scar.

Jesus is the only One of whom we are told that He was led up to be tempted. He was the leader of the race for the regaining of the blurred image, the lost mastery and dominion. He Himself bade us pray not to be so tempted. He out-matched the tempter. Any one of us, alone, is clearly out-matched by that tempter. But we may always rest secure in the victory He achieved that day. Only so are we safe.

It is noteworthy that the place of the temptation was chosen by the Spirit, and what place it is He chooses. Mark keenly, the tempter did not choose it. He was obliged to start in there, but he seized the first chance to get away to scenes more congenial to himself.

The wilderness is one of the most marked spots on the earth's crust. That remarkable stretch of land going by swift, steep descents almost from Jerusalem's very door down to the Dead Sea. It was once described as "the garden of God," that is, as Eden, for beauty and fertility, like the fertile Egyptian bottoms. For long centuries no ghastlier bit of land can be found, haggard, stripped bare, its strata twisted out of all shape, blistering peeling rocks, scorching furnace-heat reflected from its rocks, swept by hot desert winds, it is the land of death, an awful death; no life save crawling scorpions and vipers, with an occasional hyena and jackal. Here sin had a free line and ran riot. It ran to its logical conclusion, till a surgical operation – a cauterization – was necessary to save the rest. Earth's fairest became earth's ugliest. It is the one spot where sin's free swing seamed its mark deepest in. The story of sin's worst is burned into the crust of the earth with letters over a thousand feet deep. This is sin's scar: earth's hell-scar.

There is no talk of the glory of the kingdom here. Yet there had been once. This is the very spot where that proposition on smaller scale was made to a man in a crisis of his life, and where, lured by the attractive outlook, he had chosen selfishly. This is the wilderness, sin's wilderness, whither the Holy Spirit led Jesus for the tempter's assault. No man does great service for God till he gets sin into its proportion in his perspective.

Jesus was tempted. Temptation, the suggestion to wrong, must find some point of contact within. Therein consists the temptation to the man. Without doubt there was a response within to the temptations that came to Jesus. Satan always throws his line to catch on a hook inside. The physical sense of hunger responded to the suggestion of getting hold of a loaf. The unfailing breath of Jesus' life was trusting His Father. For the way a thing should be done, as well as for getting the result, He trusted His Father. This trust, underlying and permeating His whole life, furnishes the point of contact for the second temptation.

The ruling of a world righteously – not for the glory of reigning, ingrained in us, but for the world's good and betterment – was ingrained in Jesus by His birth, and fostered by His study of the Hebrew scriptures, and by the consciousness of His mission. Here is the point of contact with the third temptation. At once it is plain that there is nothing wrong here in the inward response. For instantly it was clear that a response of His will to these outer propositions would not be right, would be wrong, and so these points of contact were instantly held in check by His will.

"Every temptation" was brought, we are told: "tempted in all points." This does not mean that every particular temptation came to Jesus, but the heart, the essential, of every temptation. Every temptation that comes to us is along the line of the three that came to Him. By rejecting the first of each line He shut out its successors. By accepting the first of a series of temptations a man opens the way for the next, and so on. Temptations come on a scale descending. There are the first, the initial temptations, and then all that follow in their train. Rejecting the first stops the whole line. Not only that, but stops also the momentum, terrific, downward momentum of the whole line.

The first temptation is the door through which must pass all other temptations of that sort. If that door be opened these other temptations have a chance. If that door be kept shut, all these others are kept waiting. Temptation is always standing with its pointed toe at the crack of the door, waiting the slightest suggestion of an opening. This first temptation is always the likeliest of its class to get in. It is not always the same, of course. It is subtly chosen to suit the man. Jesus kept these doors rigidly shut, key turned, bolts pushed, bar up, chain hooked. So may we.

The tempting is to be done by "the devil." That is his strong point, tempting people. It is one way of recognizing some of his kin. It is a mean, contemptible sort of thing. He had fallen into a hole of his own digging, and would pull in everybody else. He is never constructive in his work, always destructive. Best at tearing down. Never builds up. His allies can often be told by their resemblance to him here. Jesus is to be tempted by this master-tempter. He is going to prove to all his brothers that the tempter has no power without the consent of the tempted. The door into a man has only the one knob. And that's on the inside.

Waiting the father's word.

Quite likely the form of the tempter's words suggests the upper current of Jesus' thought. "If thou be the Son of God." Jesus was likely absorbed with His peculiar relation to His Father, with all that that involved. The tempter cunningly seeks to sweep Him off of His feet by working on His mood. It is ever a favourite method with the tempter to rush a man. A flush of feeling, the mood of an intense emotion tipped over the balance with a quick motion of his, has swept many a man off his feet. But Jesus held steady. There was no unholy heat of ambition to disturb the calm working of His mind.

Why "if"? Did Satan doubt it? Is he asking proof? He gets it. Jesus did not need to prove His divinity except by continuing to be divine. He proved best that He was Son of God by being true to His Sonship. He naturally acted the part. We prove best that we are right by being right, not by accepting captious, critical propositions. The stars shine. We know they are stars by their shine. Satan would have Jesus use His divinity in an un-divine way. He was cunning. But Jesus was keener than the tempter was cunning.

"Get a loaf out of this stone. Don't go hungry. Be practical and sensible." The cold cruelty of Satan! He makes no effort to relieve the hunger. The hunger asked for bread and he gave it a stone. That is the best he has. He is a bit short on bread. He would use the physical need to break down the moral purpose. He has ever been doing just that. Sometimes he induces a man to break down his strength in religious activity. And then he takes advantage of his weakened condition. Even religious activity should be refused save at the leading of God's Spirit. It will not do simply to do good. The only safe thing is to do God's will, to be tied fast to the tether of the Spirit's leading.

Jesus could have made a loaf out of the stone. He did that sort of thing afterwards. It was not wrong to do it, since, under other circumstances, He did it. But it is wrong to do anything, even a good thing, at the devil's suggestion. He would shun the counsel of the ungodly. The tempter attacks first the neediest point, the hunger, and in so far the weakest, the likeliest to yield. Yet it was the strongest, too, for Jesus could make bread. The strongest point may become the weakest because of the very temptation the possession of strength gives to use it improperly. Strength used properly remains strength; used improperly it becomes weakness. The strong points always need guarding, that the balance be not tipped over and lost. Strength is never greater than when used rightly; never greater than when refused to the improper use. The essence of sin is in the improper use of a proper thing.

The first step toward victory over temptation is to recognize it. Jesus' quick, quiet reply here touches the human heart at once, and touches it at its neediest and most sensitive point, the need of sympathy, of a fellow feeling. He said, "Man shall not live." The tempter said, "God." Jesus promptly said, "Man." He came to be man, the Son of man, and the Brother of man. He took His place as a man that day in the Jordan water. He will not be budged from man's side. He will stay on the man level in full touch with His fellows at every step of the way.

He was giving to every man, everywhere in the world, under stress of every temptation; with every rope tugging at its fastenings, and threatening every moment to slip its hold, and the man be lost in the storm, to every man the right, the enormous staying power to say, "Jesus – a man – such a one as I – was here, and as a man resisted – and won. He is at my side. I'll lean on Him and resist too, – and win too – in the strength of His winning."

Jesus says here, "My life, my food, the supplying of my needs is in the hands of my Father. When He gives the word, I'll do: not before. I'll starve if He wishes it, but I'll not mistrust Him; nor do anything save as He leads and suggests. I'll not act at your suggestion, nor anybody's else but His. Starving doesn't begin to bother me like failing to trust would do. But I haven't the faintest idea of starving with such a Father."

"Not by bread alone, but by every word ... of God." Not by a loaf, but by a word. When a man is where God would have him, he can afford to wait patiently till God gives the word. A man is never as unsteady on his feet than when he has gone where he was not led. "I go at my Father's word." "I wait for my Father's word." Jesus' study of the parchment rolls in Nazareth was standing Him in good stead now. Through many a prayerful hour over that Word had come the trained ear, the waiting spirit, the doing of things only at the Father's initiative. He could make bread, but He wouldn't, unless the Father gave the word. It was not simply that He would not act at the tempter's suggestion, but He would not act at all except at the Father's word. And to this Jesus remained true, whether the request for evidence came from the tempter direct, or from sneering Pharisee at the temple's cleansing, or from unbelieving brothers.

Life comes not through what a man can make, but through the Father's controlling presence: not through our effort, but through the Father's power transmitted through the pipe line of our ready obedience.

"Just to let thy Father do
As He will.
Just to know that He is true,
And be still.
Just to follow hour by hour
As He leadeth.
Just to draw the moment's power
As it needeth.
Just to trust Him. This is all.
Then the day will surely be
Peaceful, whatsoe'er befall,
Bright and blesséd, calm and free."[20]

Jesus held every activity, every power subject to the Father's bidding. Not only obedient, but nothing else. Waiting the Father's send-off at every turn: this is the message from Jesus that first tug, and first victory. Jesus had held true in the realm of the body, in His relationship to Himself.

---

[20] Frances R. Havergal

Love never tests.

Satan shifts the scene. These wilderness surroundings grate on his nerves. The setting of this place, once first class, is now rather worn. He's famous at that. It's a favourite device of His; quick scene-shifting. A man wins a victory over temptation, but a quick change of surroundings finds him unprepared if he isn't ever alert for it, and down he goes before the new, unexpected rush, before he can get his wind. The tempter is not a fool, as regards man. That is, as a rule he is not. In the light of all facts obtainable about his career, that word might be thought of. Yet no man of us may apply the word to him. Not one of us is a match for him. We're not in the same class. In his keen subtlety and cunning he can outmatch the keenest of us; outwit and befool without doing any extra thinking. I am not using the word wisdom of him. We are safe only in the wisdom of our big Brother who drew his fangs in the wilderness that day.

He chooses shrewdly the spot for each following temptation. He's a master stage manager. He always works for an atmosphere that will help his purpose. He took Jesus up to one of the wings of the temple in the holy city. The holy city, and especially its temple, would awaken holiest emotions. Here it was that Jesus, as a boy, years before, had probably first caught fire. It is likely that He never forgot that first visit. Here everything spoke to Him of His Father. The tempter is skilfully following the leading of Jesus' reply. Jesus had given a religious answer. So He is given a religious atmosphere, and taken to a religious place. He would trust the Father implicitly. Here is an opportunity to let men see that beautiful spirit of trust. Here is a chance for a master-stroke. A single simple act will preach to the crowds. "You'll come down in the midst of an open-mouthed, admiring crowd." The devil loves the spectacular, the theatrical. He is always working for striking, stagy effects.

How many a man has yielded to the religious temptation! He is taken up in the air, and seems to float among ethereal clouds. It is better for us to live in the strength of Somebody else's victory, and keep good hard earth close to the soles of our feet, or we may come into contact with it suddenly with feet and head changing places.

The devil "taketh" Jesus. How could he? He could do it only by Jesus' consent. Jesus yields to his taking. He has a strong purpose in it. He was going for the sake of His brothers. The tempter cannot take anybody anywhere except with his full consent. He tries to, and often befools men into thinking he can. It's a lie. He cannot. Every man is an absolute sovereign in his will, both as regards God and Satan. God will not do anything with us without our ready consent. And be it keenly remembered that the tempter cannot. Here Jesus gave consent for His brothers' sake.

The tempter acts his part like an old hand. The proper thing here is some scripture, repeated earnestly in unctuous tones. Was it from this tempter that all of us religious folks and everybody else have gotten into the inveterate habit of quoting verse and sentence entirely out of connection? Any devil's lie can be proven from the Scriptures on that plan. If it was he who set the pace, certainly it has been followed at a lively rate. It was a cunning quotation, cunningly edited.

The angels are ministering spirits. On their hands they do bear us up. It is all true, blessedly true. But it is only true for the man who is living in the first verse of that ninety-first psalm, "in the secret place of the most High." The tempter threads his way with cautious skill among those unpleasant allusions to the serpent, and the dragon, and getting them under our feet, and then twisting and trampling with our hard heels. He knew his ground well, and avoids such rough, rude sort of talk. It was a cunning temptation, cunningly staged and worded and backed. He was doing his best. One wonders if he really thought Jesus could be tripped up that way. So many others have been, and are, even after Jesus has shown us the way. A dust cloth would help some of us – for our Bibles – and a little more exercise at the knee-joint, and a bit of the hard common sense God has given every one of us.

Did Jesus' wondrous, quiet calm nettle the tempter? Was He ever keener and quieter? He would step from the substantial boat-deck to the yielding water, He would cut Himself off from His Nazareth livelihood and step out without any resources, He would calmly walk into Jerusalem when there was a price upon His head, for so He was led by that Spirit to whose sovereignty He had committed Himself. But He would do nothing at the suggestion of this tempter. Jesus never used His power to show He had it, but to help somebody. He could not. It is against the nature of power to attempt to prove that you have it by using it. Power is never concerned about itself, but wrapped up in practical service. There were no theatricals about Jesus. He was too intensely concerned about the needs of men. There are none in God-touched men. Elisha did not smite the waters to prove that Elijah's power rested upon him, but to get back across the Jordan to where his work was needing him and waiting his touch. Jesus would wear Himself out bodily in ministering to men's needs, but He wouldn't turn a hair nor budge a step to show that He could. This is the touch-stone by which to know all Jesus-men.

He rebukes this quotation by a quotation that breathes the whole spirit of the passage where it is found. Thou shalt not test God to see if He will do as He promises. These Israelites had been testing, criticizing, questioning, doubting God. That's the setting of His quotation. Jesus says that love never tests. It trusts. Love does not doubt, for it knows. It needs no test. It could trust no more fully after a test, for it trusts fully now. Aye, it trusts more fully now, for it is trusting God, not a test. Every test of God starts with a question, a doubt, a misgiving of God. Jesus' answer to the second temptation is: love never tests. It trusts. Jesus keeps true in His relation to His Father.

The devil acknowledges the King.

Another swift shift of the scene. Swiftness is a feature now. In a moment of time, all the kingdoms, and all the glory of all the earth. Rapid work! This is an appeal to the eye. First the palate, then the emotions, now the eye. First the appetites, then the religious sense, now the ambition. The tempter comes now to the real thing he is after. He would be a god. It is well to sift his proposition pretty keenly, on general principles. His reputation for truthfulness is not very good, which means that it is very bad. Who wants to try a suspicious egg? He could have quite a number of capitals after his name on the score of mixing lies and the truth. He has a distinct preference for the flavour of mixed lies.

Here are the three statements in his proposal. All these things have been delivered unto me. I may give them to whom I will. I will give them to you. The first of these is true. He is "the prince of this world." The second is not true, because through breach of trust he has forfeited his rule, though still holding to it against the Sovereign's wish. The third is not true. Clearly he hadn't any idea of relinquishing his hold, but only of swamping Jesus. Two parts lie: one-part truth – a favourite formula of his. The lie gets the vote. A bit of truth sandwiched in between two lies.

He asks for worship. Did he really think that possibly Jesus would actually worship him? The first flush answer is, surely not. Yet he is putting the thing in a way that has secured actual worship from many a one who would be horrified at such a blunt putting of his conduct. We must shake off the caricature of a devil with pointed horns, and split hoot, and forked tail, and see the real, to understand better. From all accounts he must be a being of splendour and beauty, of majestic bearing, and dignity. His appeal in effect is this: – These things are all mine. You have in you the ingrained idea of a world-wide dominion over nature, and of ruling all men as God's King. Now, can't we fix this thing up between us? Let's be friendly. Don't let's quarrel over this matter of world dominion.

You acknowledge me as your sovereign. You rule over all this under me. I'll stand next to God, and you stand next to me. It's a mere technical distinction, after all. It'll make no real change in your being a world-wide ruler, and it will make none with me either. Each will have a fair share and place. Let's pull together. – The thing sounds a bit familiar. It seems to me I have heard it since somewhere, if I can jog up my memory. It has raised a cloud of dust in many a man's road, and blurred the clear outlines of the true plan – has raised? – is raising.

Jesus' answer is imperative. It is the word of an imperative. He is the King already in His Father's plan. He replies with the sharp, imperial brevity of an emperor, a king of kings, "Get thee hence!" Begone! The tempter obeys. He knows his master. He goes. Biting his teeth upon his hot spittle, utterly cowed, he slinks away. Only one Sovereign, Jesus says. All dominion held properly only by direct dependence upon Him, direct touch with Him, full obedience to Him. No compromise here. No mixing of issues. Simple, direct relation to God, and every other relation through that. No short cuts for Jesus. They do but cut with deep gashes the man who cuts. The "short" describes the term of his power, a short shrift.

When the devil has used up all his ammunition – That's a comfort. There is an end to the devil if we will but quietly hold on. Every arrow shot. Not a cartridge left. Yet he is not entirely through with Jesus. He has retired to reform the broken lines. He'll melt up the old bullets into different shape. They have been badly battered out of all shape by striking on this hard rock. He's a bit shaken himself. This Jesus is something new. When he can get his wind he will come back. He came back many times. Once through ignorant Peter with the loaf temptation in new shape, once through His mother's loving fears with the emotional temptation, and through the earnest, hungry Greeks, and the bread-full thousands with the kingdom temptation. Yet the edge of His sword is badly nicked, and never regains its old edge.

But now he goes. He obeys Jesus. The tempter resisted goes, weakened. He is a coward now. He fights only with those weaker than himself. He doesn't take a man of his own size. Temptation resisted strengthens the man. There is a new resisting power. There is the fine fettle that victory gives. Jesus is Victor. The Jordan experience has left its impress. Every act of obedience is to the tempter's disadvantage. In Jesus we are victors, too. But only in Him.

Through Jesus we meet a fangless serpent. The old glare is in the eye, the rattles are noisy, but the sting's out. He is still there. He still can scare; but can do not even that to the man arm-in-arm with Jesus. Jesus keeps true the relationship to all men and to nature by keeping true the relationship to His Father.

Our Father, lead us not into temptation as Jesus was led. We're no match for the tempter. Help us to keep arm-in-arm with Jesus, and live ever in the power of His victory.

The Transfiguration: An Emergency Measure

God in sore straits.

The darkest hour save only one has now come in Jesus' life. And that one which was actually darkest, in every way, from every view-point darkest, had in it some gleams of light that are not here. Jesus is now a fugitive from the province of Judea. The death plot has been settled upon. There's a ban in Jerusalem on His followers. Already one man has been cut off from synagogue privileges, and become a religious and social outcast. The southerners are pushing the fight against Jesus up into Galilee.

Four distinct times that significant danger word "withdrew" has been used in describing Jesus' departure from where the Judean leaders had come. First from Judea to Galilee, then from Galilee to distant foreign points He had gone, for a time, till the air would cool a bit. The bold return to Jerusalem at the fall Feast of Tabernacles had been attended, first by an official attempt to arrest, and then by a passionate attempt to stone Jesus to death.

And now the Galilean followers begin to question, and to leave. His enemies' northern campaign, together with His own plain teaching, has affected the Galilean crowds. They come in as great numbers as ever to hear and to be healed. But many that had allied themselves as Jesus' followers decide that He is not the leader they want. He is quite too unpractical. The kingdom that the Galileans are eager for, that the Roman yoke may be shaken off, seems very unlikely to come under such a leader. Many desert Him.

Jesus felt the situation keenly. The kingdom plan in Jerusalem had failed. And now the winning of individuals as a step in another plan is slipping its hold. These people are glad of bread and the easing of bodily distress, but the tests of discipleship they pull away from. He turns to the little band of His own choosing, with a question that reveals the keen disappointment of His heart. There's a tender yearning in that question, "Will ye also go away?" And Peter's instant, loyal answer does not blind His keen eyes to the extremity. With sad voice He says, "One of you, my own chosen friends, one of you is a – devil." Things are in bad shape, and getting worse.

It was a time of dire extremity. God was in sore straits. The kingdom plan was clearly gone for the present. The rub was to save enough out of the wreckage to get a sure starting-point for the new plan, through which, by and by, the other original plan would work out. There can be no stronger evidence of God's need of men than this transfiguration scene. Just because He had made man a sovereign in his will, God must work out all of His plans through that sovereign will. He would not lower one whit His ambition for a man free in his own will. He Himself would do nothing to mar the divine image in man. For man's sake, and through man's will – that is ever God's law of dealing.

Fire and anvil for leaders.

The great need just now was not simply for men who would be loving and loyal, but men who would be leaders. It has ever been the sorest need. Men are not so scarce, true-hearted men, willing to endure sacrifice, but leaders have always been few, and are. Nothing seems to be less understood than leadership; and nothing so quickly recognized when the real thing appears. Peter was a leader among these men. He had dash and push. He was full of impulse. He was always proposing something. He acted as spokesman. He blurted out whatever came. The others followed his lead. There were the crude elements of leadership here. But not true leadership of the finer, higher kind.

The whole purpose of the transfiguration was to get and tie up leaders. It was an emergency measure, out of the regular run of things. Goodness makes character. It takes goodness plus ability to make true leadership. The heart can make a loving follower. It takes a heart, warm and true, plus brains to make a leader. Character is the essential for life. For true leadership, there needs to be character plus ability: the ability to keep the broad sweep of things, and not be lost in details, nor yet to lose sight of details; to discern motive and drifts; to sift through the incidentals which may be spectacular and get to the essential which may be in Quaker garb[21].

There are two sorts of leadership, of action, and of thought. By comparison with the other, leaders of action are many, leaders of thought few. Peter was the leader in action of the disciples, and in the earlier church days. John became the leader in thought of the later years of the early church. Paul was both, a very unusual combination. Leaders are born, it is true. But the finest and truest and highest leaders must be both born leaders, and then born again as leaders. There needs to be the original stuff, and then that stuff hammered into shape under hard blows on the anvil of experience. The fire must burn out the clay and dirt, and then the hammer shape up the metal. Leaders must have convictions driven in clear through the flesh and bone, and riveted on the other side.

Simon loved Jesus, but there needed to be more before Peter would arrive. It took the transfiguration to put into the impulsive, unsteady, wobbling Simon the metal that would later become steel in Peter. Yet it took much more, and finally the fire of Pentecost, to get the needed temper into the steel. These same lips could give that splendid statement that has become the church's foundation; and, a bit later, utter boldly foolish, improper words to Jesus; and, later yet, utter vulgar profanity, and words far worse, aye, the worst that could be said about a friend, and in that friend's need, too.

This was a fair sample of the clay and iron, the Simon and the Peter in this man. Yet it was with painful slowness that he had been brought up to where he is now. Two years of daily contact with Jesus. Slow work! No, rapid work. Nobody but Jesus could have done it in such a short time. Nobody but Jesus could have done it at all. And, mark you keenly, this man is the leader of the band of men that stand closest to Jesus. This is the setting of the great transfiguration scene.

An irresistible plan.

Jesus goes off, away from the crowds, to have a bit of quiet time with this inner band of His. Here is the strategic point, now. The key to the future plan is in this small group. If that key can be filed into shape, cleaned of rust, and gotten to fit and turn in the lock, all may yet be well. The nub of all future growth is here. With simple, keen tact He

---

21 Quaker garb – simple, plain, ordinary…

127

begins His questionings, leading on, until Peter responds with his splendid declaration for which the church has ever been grateful to him. "Thou art the Christ, the Son of the living God." It comes to Jesus' ears as a grateful drink of cold water to a thirsty man on a hot day in a dusty road.

Then to this leader and to the inner circle, He reveals the changed plan. For the first time the word church is used, that peculiar word which later becomes the name of the new organization, "a company of persons called out." He is going to build up a church upon this statement of faith from Peter's lips, and this church will hold the relation to the kingdom of key-holder, administrator. The church is to be a part of the administration of the coming kingdom.

And so Jesus begins His difficult, sad task of preparing this band for the event six months off in Jerusalem. There is to be a tragedy before the building of the church which will hold the kingdom keys. So thoroughly does Peter fail to understand Jesus, that with stupid boldness he attempts to "rebuke" Him. Peter "took" Jesus. A great sight surely! He slips his hand in Jesus' arm and takes Him off to one side to – straighten – Him – out. This Jesus is being swept off His feet by undue emotional enthusiasm. Peter would fix it up and save the day. It would take Peter to do that.

And this is a sample of the best leadership in this inner group. Things were in bad shape. All the machinery hung upon a little pin holding two parts together. That pin threatens to bend and break for lack of temper. The Son of God leaves all else and turns aside to attend to a pin. The future of the kingdom hung upon three undisciplined country fishermen. The transfiguration spells out God's dire extremity in getting a footing in human hearts and brains for His plans. Something must be done.

Mark what that something was to be: so simple in itself, so tremendous in its results. They were to be allowed to see Jesus. That would be enough. The Jesus within would look out through the body He was using. The real Jesus within looked out through the Jesus they knew. He let these men see Himself a few moments; simply that. All of that, yet simply that. They were His lovers. They were to be sorely tried by coming events. They were to be the leaders. To love, for a time of sore need, for service's sake, for the sake of the multitudes whose leaders they were to be, for the saving of the church plan, and beyond of the kingdom plan, the Jesus within looked out for a few moments into their faces.

It was the same plan used later in getting another leader. Jesus had to go outside these men for a man with qualifications needed by the situation that these men did not have. The human element again in evidence. Paul says, "When I could not see for the glory of that light." That light bothered his eyes. The old ambitions were blurred. He couldn't see them. The outlines dimmed, the old pedigree and plans faded out. They could no longer be seen for the glory of that light. It is the plan the Master has ever used, and still does. It is irresistible.

"The glory of that light."

It was six days, or eight counting both ends, after the first telling of the coming tragedy that shook them so. Here is a bit of practical psychology. Jesus lets the brain impression made by that strange announcement deepen before making the next impression. Jesus went up into the mountain "to pray." Prayer never failed Him. It was equal to every need with Jesus. It was while praying that the wondrous change came. Changed while praying. When Moses came down from that long time alone with God, his face was full of the glory reflected from God's presence. Stephen's face caught the light of another Face into which he was intently looking.

Jesus was changed from within. It was His own glory that these men saw. He had wrapped Himself up in a bit of human tapestry so He could move among men without blinding their eyes. Now He looks out through the strands. They are astonished and awed to find that face they know so well now shining as the sun, and the garments made transparent as light, glistening like snow, by reason of the great brilliance of the light within. Yet Jesus let out only a part of the glory. When Paul saw, on the Damascus road, the light was above the shining of the sun.

When their eyes get over the first daze, the disciples come to see that besides Jesus there are two others, two of the old Hebrew leaders. There is Moses, the great maker of the nation, the greatest leader of all. And rugged Elijah, who had boldly stood in the breach and saved the day when the nation's king was proposing to replace the worship of Jehovah with demon-worship. They are talking earnestly together, these three, about – what? The great sacrifices Jesus had been enduring? The disappointment in the kingdom plan? The suffering and shame to be endured? The bitter obstinacy of the opposition? The chief priests' plotting? Listen! They are talking about the departure, the exodus, the going out and up, Jesus is about to accomplish. They are absorbed in Jesus. He was about to execute a master-stroke. He is going to accomplish a great move. They are wholly absorbed in Him, this Moses, and Elijah, and in this great move of His for men.

Meanwhile these men lying on the ground are waking up and rubbing their eyes. The only jarring note is a human note. John and James look with awe, reverent awe. It is an insight into their character that nothing is said about them. Their sense of reverence and power of control are to the front. It is dear, impulsive old Peter who can't keep still, even amid such a scene. His impulsive heart is just back of his lips, with no check-valves between. He must offer a few remarks. This great vision must be duly recognized. What a sensation it would make in Jerusalem to get these two men to stay and come down and address a meeting! That would turn the tide surely. Luke graciously explains that he did not know what he was saying. No, probably not. The tongue seemed to be going mechanically, rather than by the controlling touch of the will. Peter seems to have a large posterity, some of whom abide with us to this day.

Then the vision is shut out by the intervening cloud. This human interference disturbs the atmosphere. For Peter's sake, the glory is hidden that the impression of it may not be rubbed out even slightly by his own speech. We blur and lose the impression God would make upon us, by our speech, sometimes. A bit of divine practical psychology, this movement of the cloud. Then the quiet voice that thrilled them with the message of the Jordan, "This is My Son; My Chosen One: hear ye Him." Then it is all over.

It is most striking that this wondrous vision of glory is for these three obscure, untutored men, of lowly station. Not for the nation's leaders. Yet the reason is plain. They had gladly accepted what light had come. To them came more. Their door was open. It is these men who had obeyed light that now received more. To him that hath received what light has come shall be given more. From him that hath no light, because he won't let it in, shall be taken away even what light he has. Shut fists will stifle what is already held, and the life of it oozes out between the fingers.

In each of the three Gospels recording this scene it is introduced by the same quotation from Jesus' lips. There were some persons in His presence who would not die until they had seen the kingdom of God. The writers' reference is clearly to the vision that follows. It is said to be a vision of the coming kingdom. Jesus, with the divine glory within, no longer concealed, but shining out with an indescribable splendour, up above the earth, with two godly men, one of whom had died, and the other had been caught up from the earth without death, talking earnestly about men and affairs on the earth, and in direct communication with the Father – that is the vision here of the kingdom.

A vision of Jesus.

And so the darkest hour save only one was filled with the brightest light. The after, darker hour of Calvary had gleams of light from this transfiguration scene. There was faithful John's sympathetic presence all through the trial. John never flinched. And Peter had tears that caught the light from Jesus' eyes, and reflected their glistening rays within. Those tears of Peter's were a great comfort to Jesus that night and the next day. The two greatest leaders were sure.

The transfiguration served its purpose fully. The memory of it saved Peter out of the wreckage of Simon, else Judas' hemp might have had double use that night. Under the leadership of these men, the little band hold together during that day, so awful to them in the killing of their leader and the dashing of all their fondest hopes on which they had staked everything. Two nights later finds them gathered in a room. Could it have been the same upper room where they had eaten with Him that never-to-be-forgotten night, and listened to His comforting words? Only Thomas does not come. Everybody swings in but one. That shows good work by these leaders. But another week's work brings him, too, into the meeting and into the light.

These three men never forgot the sight of that night. John writes his Gospel under the spell of the transfiguration. "We beheld His glory" he says at the start, and understands Isaiah's wondrous writings, because he, too, "saw His glory." The impression made upon Peter deepened steadily with the years. The first impression of garments glistening beyond any fuller's skill has grown into an abiding sense of the "majesty" of Jesus and "the majestic glory." I think it wholly likely, too, that this vision of glory was in James' face, and steadied his steps, as so early in the history he met Herod's swordsman.

It was a vision of Jesus that turned the tide. There's nothing to be compared with that. A man's life and service depend wholly on the vision of Jesus that has come, that is coming. When that comes, instinctively he finds himself ever after saying, without planning to,

With the Damascus traveller he will be saying, "When I could not see for the glory of that light." May we each with face open, uncovered, all prejudice and self-seeking torn away, behold the glory of Jesus, even though for the sake of our eyes it come as a reflected glory. Then we shall become, as were Moses and Stephen, unconscious reflectors of that glory. And the crowd on the road shall find Jesus in us and want Him. Then, too, we ourselves shall be changing from glory to glory, by the inner touch of Jesus' Spirit, as we continue gazing.

Gethsemane: The Strange, Lone Struggle

The pathway in.

Great events always send messengers ahead. There is a movement in the spirit currents. A sort of tremor of expectancy affects the finer currents of air. The more sensitively organized one is, that is to say, the more the spirit part of a man dominates body and mind, the more conscious will he be of the something coming.

Jesus was keenly conscious ahead of the coming of Calvary. Apart from the actual knowledge, there was a painful thrill of expectancy, intensifying as the event came nearer. The cross cast long, dark shadows ahead. The darkest is Gethsemane. It would be, for it was nearest. But there were other shadows before that of the olive grove. Jesus plainly reveals in His behaviour, in His appearance, that He felt keenly, into the very fibre, so sensitively woven, of His being, that the experience of the cross would be a terrific one for Him. It was deliberately chosen by Him, and the time of its coming chosen in the full knowledge that it would be an awful ordeal. It would establish the earth's record for suffering, never approached before or since.

As He turns His face for the last time away from Galilee, and to Judea, it is with the calmness of strong deliberation. Yet the intenseness of the

---

[22] Mary D James – All for Jesus

inner spirit, in its look ahead, is shown in His face, His demeanour. As He comes to a certain Samaritan village on the road south, the usual invitation to stop for rest and a bit of refreshment is withheld out of respect to His evident purpose. It is clear to these villagers that His face is set to go to Jerusalem. In Luke's striking language, "His face was going to Jerusalem." What going to Jerusalem meant to Him had no meaning to them. They saw only that face, and were so caught by the strong, stern determination plainly written there that they felt impelled not to offer the usual hospitality.

They were Samaritans, it is true, a half-breed race, hated by Jews, and hating them, but invariably they had been friendly to Jesus. That must have been a marked face that held back these homely country people from pressing their small attentions upon Jesus. They are keener to read the meaning of that face than are these disciples who are more familiar with the sight of it. The impress already made upon the inner spirit by the great event toward which Jesus had determinedly set Himself was even thus early marked in His face.

Later, on that journey south, as the time and place are nearing, He strides along the road, with such a look in His face as makes these men, who had lived in closest touch, "amazed," that is, awed and frightened. And as they followed behind, they were "afraid." It is the only time it is said that the sight of His face made them afraid. Then He explains to them what is in His thoughts, with full details of the indignities to be heaped upon His person. The sternness of His purpose, perhaps not only the terrible experience of knowing sin at such close range, but, not unlikely, an anger, a hot indignation against sin and its ravages, which He was going to stab to death, flashed blinding lightning out of those eyes.

It was, not unlikely, something of the same feeling as made Him shake with indignation as He realized His dear friend Lazarus in the cold, clinging embrace of death, sin's climax. The determination to conquer sin, give it a death thrust, mingled with His acute consciousness of that through which He must go in the doing of it, wrote deep marks on His face. It is the beginning already of Gethsemane, as that, in turn, is of Calvary.

Earlier in the last week occurs the incident which agitates Jesus so, of the Greeks' request for an interview. These earnest seekers for truth, from outside the Jewish nation, seem to bring up to His mind the great outside world, so hungry for Him, and for which He was so hungry. But, quick as a flash, there falls over that the inky black shadow of a cross in

His path, and the instant realization that only through it could He get out to these great outside crowds.

As though unaware of the presence of the crowds, He begins talking with Himself, out of His heart, saying words which none understand. "Now is my innermost being agitated, all shaken up; and what decisive word shall I speak? Shall I say, 'Father, save me from this experience'? He can. No, I cannot say that, for for this purpose I have deliberately come to it. This is what I will say – and the agitation within His spirit issues in the victorious tightening of every rivet in His purpose – 'Father, glorify Thy name.'" This is Gethsemane already, both in the struggle and in the victory through loyalty to the Father's will.

The climax of Jesus' suffering.

And now comes Gethsemane. Both hat and shoes quickly go off here, for this is holiest ground. One looks with head bowed and breath held in, and reverential awe ever deepening. The shadow of the cross so long darkening His path is now closing in and enveloping Jesus. The big trees cast black shadows against the brilliance of the full moon. Yet they are as bright lights beside this other shadow, this inky shadow cast by the tree up yonder, just outside the Jerusalem wall, with the huge limb sitting sharply astride the trunk.

The scene under these trees has been spoken of by almost all, if not by all, as a strange struggle. With a great variety of explanations men have wondered why He agonized so. It was a strange struggle, and ever will be, not understood, strange to angels and to men and to demons. It is strange to angels of the upper world, for they do not know, and cannot, the terrific meaning of sin as did Jesus. It is strange to all other men except Jesus, for we do not know the meaning of purity as Jesus did. And it was strange to demons, for in the event of the morrow sin was working out a new degree of itself, a new superlative, in its final attack on Jesus. Sin was trying to strangle God. Even demons stared.

Purity refined beyond what angels knew, and sin coarsened beyond what demons knew were coming together. Purity's finest and sin's coarsest were coming together in the closest touch thus far, in this Man under those old brown-barked grey-leaved, gnarly trees. The shock of such extremes meeting would be terrific. It was terrific here under the trees. It was yet more so on the morrow. Here was the cross in anticipation. Calvary was in Gethsemane.

Man never will understand the depth of Gethsemane. We are incapable of sympathizing with Jesus here. Yet it is true that as the Holy Spirit within a man increases the purity, and the horror of sin, there comes an increasing sense of sympathy with Him, and an increasing appreciation that we cannot go into the depths of what He knew here. In the best of us sin is ingrained. Jesus was wholly free from taint or twist of sin. He knew it only in others. Now He, the pure One, purity personified, was coming into closest contact with sin, and sin at its worst. He had been in contact with sin in others. He had seen its cruel ravages and been indignant against it.

Now, on the morrow, He is to know sin by a horrid intimacy of contact, and sin at a new worst. He was yielding to its tightest hold. Sin at its ugliest would stretch out its long, bony arms and gaunt hands, and fold Him to itself in closest embrace and hold Him there. And He was allowing this, that so when sin's worst was done, He might seize it by the throat and strangle it. He would put death to death. Yet so terrific is the struggle that He must accept in Himself that which He thereby destroys. This is the agony of Gethsemane. It may be told, but not understood. Only one as pure as He could understand, and then only under circumstances that never will come again.

The horror of this contact with sin is intensified clear out of our reach by this: it meant separation from His Father. The Father was the life of Jesus. The Father's presence and approving smile were His sunshine. From the earliest consciousness revealed to us was that consciousness of His Father. Only let that smile be seen, that voice heard, that presence felt by this One so sensitive to it, and all was well. No suffering counted. The Father's presence tipped the scales clear down against every hurting thing.

But – now on the morrow that would be changed. The Father's face be – hidden – His presence not felt. That was the climax of all to Jesus. Do you say it was for a short time only? In minutes y-e-s. As though experiences were ever told by the clock! What bulky measurements of time we have! Will we never get away from the clocks in telling time? No clock ever can tick out the length to Jesus of that time the Father's face was hidden. This hiding of the Father's face was the climax of suffering to Jesus.

Alone.

It was a very full evening for Jesus. In the upper room of a friend's house they meet for the eating of the Passover meal. There is the great act of washing His disciples' feet, the eating of the old Hebrew prophetic meal, the going out of Judas into the night of his dark purpose, the new simple memorial meal. Then come those long quiet talks, in which Jesus speaks out the very heart of His heart, and that marvellous prayer so simple and so bottomless.

Very likely He is talking, as they move quietly along the Jerusalem streets, out of the gate leading toward the Kedron brook, and then over the brook toward the enclosed spot, full of the great old olive trees. The moon is at the full. This is one of His favourite praying places. He is going off for a bit of prayer. So He approaches this great crisis. There is a friendly word spoken to these men that they be keenly alert, and pray, lest they yield to temptation. It is significant, this word about temptation. Then into the woods He goes, the disciples being left among the trees, while He goes in farther with the inner three, then farther yet, quite alone. Intense longing for fellowship mingles with intense longing to be alone. He would have a warm hand-touch, yet they cannot help Him here, and may do something to jar.

Now He is on His knees, now prone, full length, on His face. The agony is upon Him. Snatches of His prayer are caught by the wondering three ere sleep dulls their senses. "My Father – if it be possible – let – this – cup – pass – from – me – Yet – Thy – will – be done." The words used to tell of His mental distress are so intense that the translators are puzzled to find English words strong enough to put in their place. A frenzy of fright, a nightmare horror, a gripping chill seizes Him with a terrible clutch. It is as though some foul, poisonous gas is filling the air and filling His nostrils and steadily choking His gasping breath. The dust of death is getting into His throat. The strain of spirit is so great that the life tether almost slips its hold. And angels come, with awe stricken faces, to minister. Even after that, some of the life, that on the morrow is to be freely spilled out, now reddens the ground. The earth is beginning to feel the fertilizing that by and by is to bring it a new life.

By and by the mood quiets, the calm returns and deepens. The changed prayer reveals the victory: "My Father, if this cup cannot pass away except I drink it – if only through this experience can Thy great love-plan for the race be worked out – Thy – will" – slowly, distinctly, with the throbbing of His heart and the iron of His will in them, come the words – "Thy – will – be – done." In between times He returns to the drowsy disciples with the earnest advice again about being awake, and alert, and praying because of temptation nearby.

And gentle reproach mingles in the special word spoken to Peter. "Simon, are you sleeping? Could you not be watching with me one hour?" Yes, this was Simon now, the old Simon. Jesus' new Peter was again slipping from view. Then the great love of His heart excuses their conduct. What masterly control in the midst of unutterable agitation! Back again for a last bit of prayer, and then He turns His face with a great calm breathing all through those deep lines of suffering, and with steady step turns toward the cross.

Calvary: Victory

Yielding to arrest.

It is probably close to midnight when Jesus steps out from among the trees to meet the crowds headed by the traitor. He knew they were coming, and quietly goes to meet them. There is a great rabble that the chief priests had drummed up, a city rabble with Roman soldiers, some of the chief priests' circle, and in the lead of all, Judas. Judas keeps up the pretence of friendship, and, advancing ahead of his crowd, greets Jesus with the usual kiss. Jesus dispels the deception at once with His question of reproach, "Betrayest thou with a kiss?" Damnable enough to betray, but to use love's token in hate's work made it so much worse. Then He yields to Judas' lips. It was the beginning of the indignities He was to suffer that night. Jesus quietly adds, "Friend, do what you have planned. Let there be no more shamming." But Judas' work is done. The silver secured under his belt is earned. He drops back into the crowd.

Jesus steps out into the clear moonlight, and faces the crowd pressing eagerly up. His is the one masterly, majestic presence. Quietly He asks, "Whom are you hunting for?" Back comes the reply, "Jesus of Nazareth." Jesus at once replies, "I am He." Again, that strange power of Jesus' presence is felt, but now more marked than ever before. The crowd falls backward and down to the ground. Soldiers, priests, crowds, Judas lying prone before Jesus! Again the question and the answer, and then the word spoken on behalf of His followers. This manifestation of power is for others this time.

Recovering themselves, the crowds press forward. The bewildered Peter makes an awkward stroke with a sword he had secured and cuts off the right ear of a man in the front of the crowd. Jesus gently stops the movement with a word. The Father would even then send twelve legions of angels if He were but to give the word. But He was not giving words of that sort, but doing what the Father wished. With a word of apology for His impetuous follower, the man's ear is restored with a touch. Surely he never forgot Jesus.

The leaders, now satisfied that Jesus will not use His power on His own behalf, seize Him and begin to bind His hands. As He yields to their touch, Jesus, looking into the faces of the Jewish leaders, said, "You hunt me and treat me as though I were a common robber. I have never tried to get away from you. But now for a while things are in your control, the control of the powers of night."

Meanwhile the disciples forsook Him and fled, except two, John and Peter. Peter followed at what he thought a safe distance. John kept along with the crowd, and went in "with Jesus." Mark tells about the attempted arrest of a young man who seemed friendly to Jesus, but in the struggle he escaped, leaving his garments behind. And so they make their way, a torch-light procession through the darkness of the night, back across the brook, up the steep slope to the city gate, and through the narrow streets to the palace of the high priest.

The real Jewish ruler.

Here Jesus is expected. Late as it is He is at once brought before Annas. Annas was an old man who had been high priest himself once, years before, and who had afterwards absolutely controlled that office through the successive terms of his sons and now of his son-in-law. He was the real leader of the inner clique that held the national reins in a clutching grip. Caiaphas was the nominal high priest. The old man Annas was the real leader. He controlled the inner finances and the temple revenues. To him first Jesus is taken. He begins a quizzical, critical examination of Jesus about disciples and teaching. Possibly he is trying to overawe this young Galilean. Jesus calmly answers. "I have taught openly, never secretly; everybody knows what my teaching has been. Why ask Me? These people all around have heard all my teaching." He was ever in the open, in sharp contrast with these present proceedings. One of the underlings of the high priest – struck – Jesus – in the face, saying, "Answerest thou the high priest so?" Jesus quietly replies, "If I have spoken something wrong tell me what it is, but if not, why do you strike Me?" Annas ignores the gross insult by one of his own men, and, probably with an exultant sneer that the disturber of the temple revenues is in his power at last, gives order that Jesus be bound and taken to his chief underling, Caiaphas.

This is the first phase of the condemnation determined upon beforehand, and the real settling of the Jewish disposition of Jesus. Still the forms had to be gone through. So Jesus is sent with the decision of Annas in the thongs on His hands to Caiaphas, high priest that year by the grace of the old intriguer Annas, and by Roman appointment. The thing must be done up in proper shape. These folks are great sticklers for proper forms.

Probably it is across a courtyard they go to another part of the same pile of buildings or palace. Caiaphas, too, is ready, unusual though the hour is. With him are several members of the senate, the official body in control of affairs. The plans have been carefully worked out. This night work will get things in shape before the dreaded crowds of the morrow can be aroused. Now begins the examination here. These plotters have been so absorbed in getting Jesus actually into their power that they seem to have over-looked the details of making out a strong case against Him. They really didn't need a case to secure their end, yet they seem to want to keep up the forms, probably not because of any remnants of supposed conscience left un-seared, but to swing the bothersome, fanatical crowds that must always be reckoned with. Now they deliberately try to find men who will lie about Jesus' words, and swear to it. They find some willing enough – money would fix that – but not bright enough to make their stories hang together. At last someone brings up a remark made three years before by Jesus about destroying the temple and rebuilding it in three days. It is hard to see how they might expect to make anything out of that, for in the remark, as they understood it, He had proposed to undertake the rebuilding of the famous structure if they should destroy it. And then they can't even agree here. Clearly they're hard pushed. Something must be done. Precious time is slipping away. The thing must be in shape by dawn if they are to get it through before the crowds get hold of it.

All this time Jesus stands in silence, doubtless with those eyes of His turned now upon Caiaphas, now on the others. His presence disturbed them in more ways than one. That great calm, pure face must have been an irritant to their jaded consciences. Suddenly the presiding officer stands up and dramatically cries out, as though astonished, "Answerest thou nothing? Canst thou not hear these charges against Thee?" Still that silence of lip, and those great eyes looking into His enemies' faces. Then comes the question lurking underneath all the time, put in the form of a solemn oath to the prisoner, "I adjure Thee by the living God, that Thou tell us whether Thou art the Christ, the Son of God." Thus appealed to, Jesus at once replies, "I am." And then, knowing full well the effect of the reply, He adds, "Nevertheless – notwithstanding your evident purpose regarding Me – the Son of Man will be sitting at the right hand of Power, and coming in the clouds of heaven, and ye shall see it."

In supposed righteous horror Caiaphas tore his garments, and cried, "What further need is there of witnesses? Behold you have heard His blasphemy. What verdict do you give?" Back come the eager cries, "He deserves death – Guilty." So the second session closes with the verdict of guilty agreed upon. Yet this was not official. The senate could meet only in daylight hours. The propriety of form they were so eager for requires them to wait until dawn should break, and then they could technically give the decisive verdict now agreed upon. While they are waiting, the intense hatred of Jesus in their hearts and their own cruel thirstings find outlet upon Jesus' person. They – spat – in – His – face, and struck Him, with open hand and shut fist. He is blind-folded, and then struck by one and another with derisive demands that He use His prophetic skill to tell who had been hitting Him. And this goes on for possibly a couple of hours before dawn permits the next step, soldiers vying with senators in doing Him greatest insult.

Held steady by great love.

Meanwhile a scene is being enacted within ear-shot of Jesus that hurts Him more than these vulgar insults. Peter is getting into bad shape. John was acquainted in the high priest's house-hold, and, going directly in without striking his colours, is not disturbed. Peter gets as far as the gateway, leading through a sort of alley into the open courtyard, around which on the four sides the palace was built. Here, as a stranger, he was refused admittance, until John comes to speak a word for him. In the centre of the open court a fire was burning to relieve the cold of the night, and about this was gathered a mixed crowd of soldiers and servants and attendants. Peter goes over to the fire, and, mingling with the others, sits warming himself, probably with a studied carelessness. The maid who let him in, coming over to the fire, looks intently into his face, and then says, "You belong to the Nazarene, too." Peter stammers out an embarrassed, mixed up denial, "I don't know what you mean – I don't understand – what do you say?"

Taken unawares, poor Peter mingles a lie with the denial. As soon as possible he moves away from the fire toward the entrance. It's a bit warm there – for him. He remembered afterwards that just then the crowing of a cock fell upon his ear. Again one of the serving-maids notices him and says to those standing about, "This man was with Jesus." This time the denial comes sharp and fiat, "I don't know the man." And to give good colour to his words, and fit his surroundings, he adds a bit of profanity to it.

An hour later, as he moves uneasily about, he is standing again by the fire. Something about him seems to make him a marked man. Evidently he has been talking, too. For now a man looking at him, said, "You belong to this Jesus. I can tell by the twist of your tongue." Peter promptly says, "No." Lying comes quicker now. But at once another speaks up, who was kin to the man that temporarily lost his ear through Peter's sword. "Why," he said, "certainly I saw you with Him in the garden." Again the denial that he knew Jesus mingled freely with curses and oath. And even as he spoke the air was caught again with the cock's shrill cry. And then Jesus, in the midst of the vulgarity being vented upon Him, turned those wondrous eyes upon Peter. What a look must that have been of sorrow, of reproach, and of tenderest love. It must surely have broken Peter's heart. The hot tears rushing up for vent were his answer. Those tears caught the light of love in that look, as he goes away into the night and weeps bitterly. Those bitter tears were as small, warm rain to a new growth within.

An obstinate roman.

And now the impatient leaders detect the first streaks of grey coming up in the east. The national council can now properly meet. Like their two chiefs, these men are prompt. The whips had been out over the city drumming up the members for this extraordinary session. There seems to have been a full attendance. Jesus, still bound, is led through the streets; followed by the mixed rabble, to the meeting hall, probably in the neighbourhood of the temple. He is brought in and faces these men. How some of those eyes must have gloated out their green leering! Here are the men He had not hesitated to denounce openly with the severest invective ever spoken.

Some time is spent in consultation. The difficulty here is to fix upon a charge upon which they can themselves agree, and which will also be sufficient for the desired action by the Roman governor. It was a tough task. They fail in it. These men divided into groups that were ever at swords' points. There were utter opposites in beliefs and policies. But their common hate of Jesus rises for the time above their hatred for each other. The charge must appeal to Pilate, for only he has power of capital punishment, and nothing but Jesus' blood will quench their thirst.

Their consultation results in another attempt to question Jesus in the hope of getting some word that can be used. The president goes back to his former question, "If Thou art the Christ, tell us." Jesus reminds them of the lack of sincerity in their questionings. They would not believe Him, nor answer His questions. Then He repeats the solemn words spoken in the night session, "From henceforth shall the Son of Man be seated at the right hand of the power of God." Eagerly they all blurt out, "Art Thou then the Son of God?" Back comes the quiet, steady reply, "Ye say that I am," equal to a strong yes. Instantly they decide fully and formally upon His condemnation. So closes the third phase of the Jewish examination. The death sentence is fixed upon. The thing has been formally fixed up. The ground is now cleared for taking Him to Pilate for His death sentence.

It is still early morning when Jesus is taken to Pilate. It was an imposing procession of the leading men of the nation, headed very likely by Caiaphas, that now led Jesus across the city, through its narrow streets, up to the palace of the Roman governor. Jesus is conducted into Pilate's hall of judgment within, but, with their scrupulous regard for the letter of their law, these principals would not enter his palace on that day, but remained without. They seem to be expecting Pilate to send the prisoner back at once with their death sentence endorsed.

To their surprise and disgust, Pilate comes out himself and wants to know the charge against the prisoner. They are not prepared for this. It is their weak point, and has been from the first. Their bold, sullen answer evades the question, while insisting on what they want, "If He were not a criminal we would not have brought Him to thee." They didn't want his opinion, but his power, his consent to their plot. But Pilate doesn't propose to be used as such a convenience. With scorn he tells them that if they propose to judge the case they may. This wrings from them the humiliating reminder that the power of capital punishment is withheld from them by their Roman rulers, and nothing less will satisfy them here. Then they begin a series of verbal charges. They are all of a political nature, for only such would this Roman recognize. This man had been perverting the nation, forbidding tribute to Caesar and calling Himself a King.

It takes no keenness for Pilate to see the hollowness of this sudden loyalty to Caesar. He returns to the beautiful marble judgment hall, and has Jesus brought to him again. He looks into Jesus' face. He is keen enough to see that here is no political schemer. At most probably a religious enthusiast, or reformer, or something as harmless from his standpoint. "Art Thou the King of the Jews?" he asks. Jesus' answer suggests that there was a kindliness in that face. If there be a desire for truth here He will satisfy it. This political charge had been made outside while He was within. "Do you really want to know about Me, or are you merely repeating something you have heard?" He asks, with a gentle earnestness.

But Pilate at once repudiates any personal interest. "Am I a Jew?" he asks, with plain contempt on that word. "Thine own people are accusing thee. What hast Thou done?" Then comes that great answer, "My kingdom is not of this world, if so I would be resisting these leaders and these present circumstances would all be different. But my kingdom is not of your sort or theirs." Again there likely came a bit of softening and curious interest in Pilate's face, as he asks, "Art Thou really a King then?" Jesus replies, "To this end have I been born, and to this end am I come into the world, that I should bear witness to the truth. Every one that is of the truth heareth my voice." Pilate wonders what this has to do with being a king. With a weary, impatient contempt, he says, "Truth? What is that?" The accused seems to be an enthusiast, a dreamer, yet withal there certainly was a fine nobility about Him. Certainly He was quite harmless politically.

Leaving Him there, again he goes to the leaders waiting impatiently outside. To their utter astonishment and rage he says, "I find no fault in this man." It is the judgment of a keen, critical, worldly Roman; an acquittal, the first acquittal. The waiting crowd bursts out at once in a hot, fanatical tumult of shouted protests. Is all their sleepless planning to be disturbed by this Roman heathen? The prisoner was constantly stirring up the people all through Judea and Galilee. He was a dangerous man. Looking and listening, with his contempt for them plainly in his face, and yet a dread of their wild fanaticism in his heart, Pilate's ear catches that word Galilee. "Is the man a Galilean?" "Yes." Well, here's an easy way of getting rid of the troublesome matter. Herod, the ruler of Galilee, was in the city at his palace, come to attend the festival. It would be a bit of courtesy that he might appreciate to refer the case to him, and so it would be off his own hands. And so the order is given.

A savage duel.

Once more Jesus is led through these narrow streets, with the jeering rabble ever increasing in size and the national heads in the lead. They are having a lot of wholly unexpected trouble, but they are determined not to be cheated of their prey. And now they are before Herod. This is the murderer of John. He is glad to see Jesus. There has been an eager curiosity to see the man of whom so much was said, and he hoped to have his morbid appetite for the sensational satisfied with a display of Jesus' power. He plies Him with questions, while the chief priests with fierce vehemence stand accusing Him, and asking for His condemnation.

But for this red-handed man Jesus has no word. To him rare light had come and been recognized, and then had been deliberately put out beyond recall. He has gone steadily down into slimiest slush since that. Now, with studied insolence, he treats this silent man with utmost contempt. His soldiers and retainers mock and deride, dressing Him in gorgeous apparel in mockery of His kingly claims. When they weary of the sport He is again dismissed to Pilate, acquitted. It is the second mocking and the second acquittal.

Again the weary tramping of the streets, with the chief priests' rage burning to the danger point. Twice they have been foiled. Now the matter must be forced through, and quickly, too, ere the crowd that are friendly have gotten the news. They hurry Jesus along and make all haste back to Pilate. Now begins the sixth and last phase of that awful night. Things now hasten to a climax. The character of Pilate comes out plainly here. He really feared these wildly fanatical Jews whom he ruled with a contemptuous disgust undisguised. Three times since his rule began their extreme fanaticism had led to open riot and bloodshed, and once to an appeal to the emperor, by whose favour he held his position. His hold of the office was shaky indeed if the emperor must be bothered with these superstitious details about their religion. The policy he pursued here was but a piece of the whole Roman fabric. Yet had he but had the rugged strength to live up to his honest conviction. But then, that is the one question of life everywhere and always. He failed in the test, as do thousands. Unconsciously he was touching the quivering centre of a whole world's life, and so his action stands out in boldest outline.

He comes out now and sums up the case. He had examined the prisoner and found no fault touching their charges of perverting the people. Herod, their own native ruler, who was supposed to know thoroughly their peculiar views, had also fully acquitted Him. Now, as a concession to them, he will disgrace this man by a public scourging and let him go as harmless. Instantly the air is filled with their fierce shrill cries, "Away with Him: Away with Him."

But Pilate seems determined to do the best he can for Jesus, without risking an actual break with these fanatical Orientals such as might endanger his own position. It was usual at feast times to release to the people someone who had been imprisoned for a political offense. The crowds, prompted by the chief priests, doubtless, begin to ask for the usual favour. Pilate brings forward a man named Barabbas, who was a robber and murderer and charged with leading an insurrection against Roman rule. Meanwhile, as he waits, a messenger comes up to him and repeats a message from his wife. She has been suffering much in dreams and urges that he has nothing to do with "that righteous man."

Apparently Pilate brings forward the two men, the one a robber and murderer, the other with purity and goodness stamped on every line of His face. It is a dramatic moment. "Which of the two will you choose?" he asks. It is the appeal of a heathen to the better nature of these Jews, called the people of God. Quick as a flash of lightning the word shot from their lips and into his face, "Barabbas!" "What, then, shall I do with Jesus, who is called Christ?" He is weakening now. His question shows it. They are keen to see it and push their advantage. Again the words shoot out as bullets from their hot lips, "Crucify Him: crucify Him." Still he withstands them. "Why? What evil has He done? I find no fault in Him. To please you I will chastise Him and release Him." But they have him on the run now. At once the air is filled with a confused jangle of loud shrill voices, "Away with Him! Give us Barabbas! Crucify! Crucify."

Apparently he yields. Barabbas is released. Jesus is led away to be scourged by the soldiers. His clothing is removed, and He is bent over, with thongs on the wrists drawn down, leaving the bare back uppermost and tense. The scourging was with bunches of leather strips with jagged pieces of bone and lead fastened in the ends. The blows meant for the back, even if laid on by a reluctant hand, would strike elsewhere, including the face. But reluctance seems absent here. Then occurs another, a third of those scenes of coarse vulgarity, horrid mocking, based on His kingly claims. The whole band of soldiers is called. Some old garments of royal purple are put upon Jesus. One man plaits a crown of the thorns that grow so large in Palestine, and with no easy gesture places it upon His head. A reed is placed in His hand. Then they bow the knee in turn, with "Hail! King of the Jews," and spit in His face, and rain blows down upon the thorn-crown. All the while their coarse jests and shouts of derisive laughter fill the air. Surely one could never tell the story were he not held in the grip of a strong purpose.

But now Pilate springs a surprise. The scourging might be preliminary to crucifixion or a substitute. Again Jesus is brought forward, as arrayed by the mocking soldiers. There must have been an unapproachable majesty in that great face, as so bedecked, with the indescribable suffering lines ever deepening, He stands before them with that wondrous calm still in those sleepless eyes. Pilate seems caught by the great spirit of Jesus dominant under such treatment. He points to Him and says, "Behold the Man!" Surely this utter humiliation will satisfy their strange hate.

Realizing that their fight is not yet won as they had thought, they make the air hideous with their shouts, "Crucify – crucify – crucify." Anger and disgust crowd for place in Pilate, as, with a contemptuous sneer, he says, "You crucify Him. I find no fault in Him." It would be illegal, but it would not be the first illegal thing. But these men are bound to get all they want from their weakening governor. One of the leaders sharply spoke up, "We have a law, and by our law He ought to die because He pretends to be the Son of God." The Roman custom was to respect the laws of their subject-peoples. All pretence of a political charge is now gone.

Pilate is startled. The sense of fear that has been strong with him intensifies. That face of Jesus had impressed him. His wife's message disturbed him. Now that inward feeling that this man was being wronged grips him anew. At once he has Him led into his judgment hall for another private interview. Looking into that face again with strangely mingling emotions, he puts the question, "Whence art Thou?" But those lips refuse an answer. The time for speech is past. Angered by the silence on the part of the man he had been moved to help, Pilate hotly says, "Speakest Thou not to Me? Knowest Thou not I have the power to release or to crucify?" Then this strangely masterful Man speaks in very quiet tones, as though pitying His judge, "Thou wouldst have no power against Me, except it were given thee from above: therefore he that delivered Me unto thee hath greater sin."

Again Pilate comes out to the waiting crowd more determined than ever to release Jesus. But the leaders of the mob take a new tack. They know the governor's sensitive nerve. "If thou release this man thou art not Caesar's friend. Every one that maketh himself a king speaketh against Caesar." That word "Caesar" was a magic word. Its bur catches and sticks at once. It was their master-stroke. Yet it cost them dear. Pilate instantly brings Jesus out and sits down on the judgment seat. The thing must be settled now once for all. As Jesus again faces them he says, "Behold! – your King." Again the hot shouts, "Away – Away – Crucify – Crucify." And again the question. "Shall I crucify your King?"

Now comes the answer, wrung out by the bitterness of their hate, that throws aside all the traditional hopes of their nation, "We have no king but Caesar." Having forced that word from their lips, Pilate quits the prolonged duelling.

Yet to appease that inner voice that would not be stilled – maybe, too, for his wife's sake, he indulges in more dramatics. He washes his hands in a basin of water, with the words, "I am innocent of the blood of this righteous man. See ye to it." Back come the terrible words, "His blood be on us and on our children." Surely it has been! Then Jesus is surrendered to their will. They have gotten what they asked, but at the sacrifice of their most fondly cherished national tradition and with an awful heritage. Pilate has yielded, but held them by the throat in doing it to compel words that savagely wounded their pride to utter. The savage duel is over.

Victory.

Jesus is turned over to the soldiers for the execution of the sentence. His own garments are replaced, and once more He is the central figure in a street procession, this time carrying the cross to which He has been condemned. His physical strength seems in danger of giving way under the load, after the terrible strain of that long night. The soldiers seize a man from the country passing by and force him to carry the cross. As they move along, the crowd swells to a great multitude, including many women. These give expression to their pitying regard for Jesus.

Turning about, Jesus speaks to them in words that reveal the same clear mind and masterly control as ever. "Daughters of Jerusalem, be weeping for yourselves and your babes, rather than for Me. The days are coming when it shall be said, 'Blessed are the barren, and the womb that never bare, and the breasts that never gave suck.' If they have done these things while the sap of national life still flows, what will be done to them when the dried-up, withered stage of their national life is reached!"

Now the chosen place is reached, outside the city wall, probably a rise of ground, like a mound or small hill. And the soldiers settle down to their work. There are to be two others crucified at the same time. A drink of stuff meant to stupefy and so ease the pain of torture was offered Jesus, but refused. And now the cross is gotten ready. The upright beam is laid upon the ground handy to the hole in which the end of it will slip, and the cross-piece is nailed in place. Jesus is stripped and laid upon the cross with His arms, outstretched on the cross-piece. A sharp-pointed spike is driven through the palm of each hand and through the feet. The hands are also tied with ropes as additional security. There is a small piece half-way up the upright where some of the body's weight may be supported.

As the soldiers drive the nails, Jesus' voice is heard in prayer, "Father, forgive them; they know not what they do." Then strong arms seize the upper end, and, lifting, shift the end of the cross into the hole, and so steady it into an upright position. It is nine o'clock, and the deed has been done. The soldiers, having finished their task, now go after their pay. Jesus' garments are divided up among them, but when the outer coat is reached it is found to be an unusually good garment, woven in one piece. It was the love gift of some friend likely. So they pitch dice, and in a few moments one of them is clutching it greedily as his own.

As quickly as the cross is in position the crowds are reading the inscription which has been nailed to the top to indicate the charge against the man. It was in three languages, Latin the official tongue, Greek the world tongue, and Aramaic the native tongue. Every man there read in one or other of these tongues, "The King of the Jews." Instantly the Jewish leaders object, but Pilate contemptuously dismisses their objection. This inscription was his last fling at them. And so Jesus was crucified as a King. There He is up above them all, while the great multitude stands gazing.

Now begins the last, coarse, derisive jeering. Some of the crowd call out to Jesus, "Thou that destroyest the temple, and buildest it in three days, save Thyself; if Thou art the Son of God, come down from the cross." The chief priests have dignified the occasion with their presence. Now they mockingly sneer out their taunts, "He saved others; but He can't save Himself. He is the King of Israel. Let Him come down from the cross and we will believe on Him." The two others hanging by His side, in their pain and distress, join in the taunting cries, and the soldiers add their jibes.

But through it all Jesus is silent. There He hangs with those eyes watching the people to whom His great heart was going out, for whom His great life was going out, calm, majestic, masterful, tender. The sight affects at least one of those before unfriendly. The man hanging by His side is caught by this face and spirit. He rebukes the other criminal, reminding him that they were getting their just deserts, but "This Man hath done nothing amiss." Then turning so far as he could to Jesus, he said, with a simplicity of faith that must have been so grateful to Jesus, "Jesus, remember me when Thou comest in Thy kingdom." Instantly comes the reply, "Verily, I say unto thee, to-day shalt thou be with Me in Paradise."

In the crowds were many of Jesus' personal acquaintances, including women from Galilee. Close by the cross stood His mother and aunt and faithful John and a few others of those dear to Him. Most likely John is supporting Jesus' mother with his arms. Turning His eyes toward the group, Jesus speaks to His mother in tones revealing His love, "Woman, behold thy son;" and then to John, "Behold thy mother." So He gives His mother a son to take His own place in caring for her, and to His friend John this heritage of love. John understands, and from that hour the ties between these two were of the closest and tenderest sort.

So the hours drag along until noon. And now a strange thing occurs that must have had a startling effect. At the time of day when the sunlight is brightest a strange darkness came over all the scene, the sun's light being obscured or failing wholly. And for three hours this strange, weird spectacle continues. Then the hushed silence is broken by an agonizing cry from the lips of Jesus, "My God – My God – why – didst – Thou – forsake – Me?" One of the bewildered bystanders thinks He is calling for Elijah, and another wonders if something startling will yet occur.

Jesus speaks again – "I – thirst" and some one near by with sponge and stick reaches up to moisten His lips. Then a shout, a loud cry of victory bursts in one word from those lips, "It is finished." Then softly breathing out the last words, "Father, into Thy hands I commend My spirit," and bowing His head, Jesus, masterful, kingly to the last, yielded up His spirit.

The Resurrection: Gravity Upward

A new morning.

It was near the dawning of a new morning, the morning of a new day destined to be a great day. While yet dark there come a number of women out of the city gate toward the tomb where Jesus' body had been laid. They carry spices and ointment. With woman's ever tender thoughtfulness they are bent upon some kindly service for that precious body. They had followed up the burial and noted the arrangements with a view to this morning's early service. Their whole thought is absorbed with a tomb and a body and a bit of loving attention. They wonder as they come along whom they can get to roll the heavy stone over into its groove at the side of the opening. Mary Magdalene is in the lead. With her in the darkness is her friend Mary, the mother of John and James. Others come along a little behind, in small groups.

As they get near to the place the keen eyes of Mary Magdalene notice at once with a quick start that the stone is rolled away. Somebody has been tampering with the tomb in the night. Leaving her companion, she starts back on a run into the city and finds Peter, and tells him that the Lord has been taken away, and they don't know where He has been laid. Peter, too, is startled. He gets John, and the two start back on a run.

Meanwhile the other women have gone on toward the tomb. As they approach they are startled and awed to find a man there, with the glorious appearance of an angel, sitting upon the stone. To these awe-stricken women this angel being quietly said, "Do not be afraid. I know you are looking for Jesus who was crucified. He is not here. He is risen, as He told you. Come and see the place where He lay." And as they gaze with wide open eyes, he adds, "Go quickly and tell His disciples, and be sure you tell Peter, that He is risen from the dead, and lo, He goeth before you into Galilee. You will meet Him there. Lo, I have told you." But the women were panic-stricken, and ran away down the road, and told no one except some of the apostles. And to them their story seemed ridiculous. They refused to believe such talk.

And now Peter and John come breathless to the tomb. John is in the lead. Either he is younger or swifter of foot. As he comes up he stops at the opening of the tomb, and, with a bit of reverential awe, gazes within. He can see the linen cloths lying; but the body they had encased is clearly not in them. Peter comes up, and steps at once inside for a closer inspection. There the linen cloths are, just as they had enswathed the body, but flattened down, showing the absence of anything inside their folds. The napkin that had been about the head was folded up neatly and laid over to one side. Then John enters, and as he continues looking conviction comes to him that Jesus has indeed risen. Wondering greatly at this thing, wholly unexpected by them, they go off to their homes in the city.

And now another little group of the women come up, and are perplexed in turn as the others, the stone away, the body of Jesus not there. As they stand with staring eyes and fearing hearts, two men unexpectedly appear in clothing that dazzles the women's eyes. Frightened, they bow down before these men, who seem to be angels. But the men quickly reassure them with their words. Why were they seeking a living One in a tomb? Jesus was not there. He was risen. And they remind the women of Jesus' own words about being killed and then rising again. As the men talk the women remember the Master's words, and wonderingly see their meaning now, and hurry away to tell their friends the great news.

Jesus seeking out peter.

And now Mary Magdalene has gotten back to the tomb. In her zeal for the safety of that precious body, she had made quite a journey into the city and back. Her zeal took her quickly to Peter. Her sorrow makes the way back longer. She had been first to come, but had not heard the news that came to her companions. Now she stands at the open tomb weeping. She stoops and looks in to see if it can be really true that He is not there. To her surprise two angel beings are seated, one at each end of where Jesus' body had been lying. They say to her, "Why are you weeping?" She replies, "Because they have taken away my Lord, and I know not where they have laid Him." Turning back in her grief as the words are spoken, she sees someone else standing. Again the same question by this One. Why was she weeping? Whom was she looking for? Her eyes are blinded with the rain of tears. This is likely the man in charge of the garden wherein this family tomb was.

With earnest tones she says, "Sir, if thou didst carry Him away, tell me where thou didst lay Him and I will have Him taken away." Then that one word came to her ears, her name, in that unmistakable voice, "Mary." Quicker than a flash came the response, "Oh, my Master!" That same wondrous, quiet voice continues, "Do not continue to be clinging to Me. I am not yet ascended to my Father. Be going to my brethren and tell them I ascend to My Father and your Father, My God and your God." And Mary quickly departs on her glad errand for Him. She was the first to see His face and hear His voice, and have her hand upon His person, and do something at His bidding.

And now the other women who had been at the tomb in the garden and fled away are on the road approaching the city. As they hurry along, to their utter amazement – here is Jesus in the road approaching them. With a glad smile in His eyes, the old, sweet voice speaks out in rich tones the usual simple salutation of greeting, "Good morning." At once they are down on their knees and faces, holding His feet and worshipping. And Jesus softly says, "Do not be afraid. Go tell my brethren to meet Me in Galilee, up by the old blue waters of the sea."

While these incidents were occurring, all in such short time, something else is going on of a different sort. The Roman soldiers guarding that tomb had had a great shock. They had been suddenly displaced by another guard. The sacred Roman seal had been ruthlessly broken, the stone rolled back from the opening, and someone sat upon it. Their bewildered, stupefied senses heard the movements and were aware of a strange, blinding light. Then they knew that the body they were to guard was no longer within. That was about as much as they could get together. They hurry to town and tell the chief priests. Quickly the chief priests gather their clique to confer about this new phase. Was there ever such mulish obstinacy? No thought of candid investigation seems to enter their mind. The way of covering this new difficulty is after all easy. Money will buy the soldiers, and they will do as they are bid. It took a good bit of gold. The soldiers probably were keen to know how to work so good a mine. And the story was freely circulated that the body was stolen while the soldiers slept.

Peter has gone down the road from the garden toward the city after having satisfied Himself that Jesus was not in the tomb. He was wondering what all this meant. John, lighter of foot, had hurried ahead to his home in the city, very likely to tell the news to Jesus' mother, his own new mother. Peter plods slowly along. There is no need of haste now. He is thinking, wondering, thinking. It was still early morning, with the sweet dew on the ground, and the air so still. Down past some big trees maybe he was walking, deeply absorbed, when – Somebody is by his side. It is the Master! But we must leave them alone together. That was a sacred interview, meant only for Peter.

Made known in the breaking of bread.

The news now quickly spread; the two stories, that of the soldiers, that of the disciples. Folks listened to the one they preferred. Everybody was discussing this new startling appendix to the crucifixion. A bit later in the day two others were walking along one of the country roads leading out of the city, toward a village a few miles away. They jog along slowly as men who are heavy footed with disappointment. They are intently absorbed in conversation, eagerly discussing and questioning about something that clearly puzzled them.

A Stranger, unrecognized, overtakes them and joins in their conversation. He asks, "What is this that you are so concerned about?" So absorbed are they with their thoughts, that at His question they stand still, looking sad and unable for a moment to answer. Where would they begin where there was so much? Then one of them says, "Do you lodge by yourself in the city, and even then do not know the things that have been going on there?" The Stranger draws them out. "What things?" He says. Thus encouraged, they find relief in unburdening their hearts. It was all about Jesus, a man of great power in word and deed, before God and all the people; the great cruelty with which the rulers had secured a sentence of death for Him – and – crucified – Him.

"We were, however, hoping," they said, "that He was the One who was about to redeem the nation. And now it is the third day since these things occurred. And most surprising word was brought by certain women that has greatly stirred us. They went early to the tomb, and did not find His body, but saw a vision of angels who positively said that He was alive. And some of our party went there and found it true as the women said. But – they did not see Him."

Then the Stranger began speaking in a quiet, earnest way that caught them at once. "O foolish men, so slow you are in heart to believe the messages of the old prophets! Was it not needful that the Christ should suffer these very things and to enter into His glory?" Then He began freely to quote passages from all through their sacred writings. As they walk along listening to this wonderful explanation, which now sounds so simple from this Man's lips, they come up to their home in the village. The Stranger seemed inclined to go on. But they earnestly urge Him to come in and get some refreshment and stay overnight. He may talk more. They have heard no such winsome talk since Jesus was with them.

He yields. And, as they gather over the simple evening meal, the Stranger picks up the loaf, and looking up repeats the simple grace, and breaking the loaf reaches the pieces over. But as their hands go out for the bread, their eyes turn toward the Stranger's face. Instantly they are spell-bound – that face – why – it is the Master!! Then He is not there. And they said to each other, "Did you ever hear such talking?"

"My heart was burning all the time He was talking." "And mine, too." Then they hasten back to the city. Those miles are so much shorter now! They go straight to the house where they have been meeting.

"Even So Send I You."

Here were gathered most of the apostles and several others. Eagerly they were discussing the exciting news of the day. Some know that Jesus has risen. Mary Magdalene, with eyes dancing, says, "I saw Him." But some are full of doubt and questionings. How could it be? The door is guarded, for if the frenzy of the national leaders should spread, they come next. There's a knock at the door. Cautiously it is opened. Two dusty but radiant faces appear. "The Lord is risen indeed," they exclaim. And then they tell the story of the afternoon and His wondrous explanation and of that meal.

As they are talking, all at once – who's that? – right in their midst. It looks like Jesus. There is that face with those unmistakable marks. And you can see their eyes quickly searching between the sandal straps. Yes, it looks like Him. But it can't be. Their eyes befool them. It's been a hard day for them. It must be a spirit. As they start back, there comes in that voice they can never forget, the old quiet "Good evening." – "Peace unto you." Then He holds out His hands and feet, saying, "Do not be troubled – it is I Myself – handle Me, and make sure. A spirit does not have flesh and bones as you see that I have." Then He said, "Have you something to eat?" and He ate a bit of broiled fish.

Reassured by such simple practical evidence, a glad peace fills their hearts and faces. They talk together a bit. Then Jesus rising, said again, "Peace unto you – as the Father hath sent Me, even so send I you." Then He breathed strongly upon them, saying in very quiet, solemn tones, "Receive ye the Holy Spirit – Whosesoever sins ye forgive they are forgiven. Whosoever ye retain they are retained." And again, as they look, He is not there.

But one man was absent that new Sabbath evening hour. Thomas simply could not believe, and would not, without the sanest, common-sense evidence. He missed much by not being at that meeting. The next Sabbath evening he is present with the others. Again the Master comes as before, unexpectedly standing in their midst, as they talk together about Him. And now Thomas is fully satisfied after his week of doubting. Some of us folks will always be grateful for Thomas.

Sometime later, there occurs that second wondrous draught of fishes, at the command of the unrecognized Stranger, one morning at the breaking of the day, and the talk with Peter and the others as they walk along the old shore of the sea. And to James, who seems to have been a leader by dint of a strong personality, He appears.

And one day when there was an unusually large meeting of His followers, as many as five hundred, He came as before and was recognized. And then at the last upon Olives' top came the goodbye meeting and message.

It is surely worthy of remark that the Bethany home is not represented at either cross or tomb. Many of His dear friends are named in connection with both, but not these. Here are some of those dearest to Him, and to whom He is most dear. Here is one, a woman, who had discerned more keenly ahead than any other that He was to die and why. She had understood the minor strains of the old Hebrew oratorio as none other. She had learned at His feet. And here, too, was one who knew death, and the life beyond, and then a return again to this life. It was not indifference that kept them away. They loved tenderly, and were tenderly loved. Their absence is surely most significant. Mary's ointment had already been used. This morning in glad ecstasy of spirit she and her brother and sister wait. They know.

Gravity upward.

Two things stand out very clearly about Jesus' resurrection. It was not expected by these followers, but received at first with incredulity and doubt and stubborn unwillingness to accept it without clear undisputable proof. And then that they were thoroughly satisfied that He was actually back again with them, with His personal identity thoroughly established; so satisfied that their lives were wholly controlled by the consciousness of a risen Jesus. Sacrifice, suffering, torture, and violent death were yielded to gladly for His sake.

A new morning broke that morning, the morning of a new day, a new sort of day. That resurrection day became a new day to them and to all Jesus' followers. The old Sabbath day was a rest-day. God Sabbathed from His work of creation. This new day is more, it is a victory-day. Every new coming of it spells out Jesus' victory over sin and death and our victory in Him. The old Hebrew rest-day came at the week's close. The new victory-day comes at the week's beginning. With the fine tingle of victory in our spirits we are ever at the beginning of a new life and new victory and great things to come.

Did Jesus rise? Or, was He raised? Both are said of Him. Both are true. He was raised by the power of the Father. Every bit of His human life was under the direction and control of His Father. Every act of His from first to last was in the strength of the Father. This last act was so. The Father's vindication of His Son was seen in the power that raised Him up from out of the domain of death. He was raised.

Jesus rose from the dead. The action was in accord with the law of His life. He rose at will by the moral gravity of His character. He had gone down, now He lets Himself rebound up. The language used of His death is very striking. No one of the four descriptions of the death upon the cross says that He died. The words commonly used to describe the death of others are not used of Jesus. Very different language is used. Matthew says, "He dismissed His spirit." Mark and Luke each say, "He breathed out" His life. John says, "He delivered up His spirit."

His dying was voluntary. Not only the time of it and the manner of it, but the fact of it was of His own choosing. The record never suggests that death overcame Him. He yielded to it of His own strong accord. He was not overcome by death. He could not be, for sin having no hold within His being, death could have none. Physical death is one of the logical results of the sin within. Jesus yielded up His spirit. It was a free, voluntary act. He had explained months before that so it would be. "I lay down My life that I may take it again. No man taketh it from Me, but I lay it down of Myself. I have the power to lay it down, and I have the power to take it again. This commandment I received from My Father." This being so, the return to life followed the same voluntary course. Having accomplished the purpose in dying, He now recalled His spirit into the body and rises by His own choice.

Man's true gravity is toward a centre upward. Sin's gravity is toward a centre downward. When an ordinary man, a sinful man, dies, he is overcome by the logical result of the sin in himself. He is overcome by the moral gravity downward of His sin. He has no choice. His own moral gravity apart from sin is upward. But that is overbalanced by the downward pull of the sin ingrained in his very being. And this quite apart from his attitude toward the sin.

In Jesus there was no sin. Being free of it, He rose at will. "It was not possible that He should be held by death," for it had no hold upon Him. His gravity was upward. For a purpose, a great strong purpose, He yielded to death's embrace. Now that purpose being achieved, He quietly lets Himself up toward the natural centre of gravity of His life.

The life side of death.

Clearly Jesus' body had undergone changes through death and resurrection. It is the same to outer appearance, so far as personal identity is concerned. The doubting, questioning disciples handle His person, they know His face, they recognize His voice. He eats with them and talks with them and moves in their midst as before. Even the doubter, stubborn in his demand for tangible, physical evidence, is convinced by the feel of his hands that this is indeed Jesus back again. Further, He moves about among them unrecognized till He chooses to be known. Yet this may have been His power over them rather than any changed quality in His person.

But mark that the limitations of space and of material obstructions are gone after the resurrection. He no longer needs to get that body through space by physical strength or management, but seems to go where He will by choosing to be there. He is no longer affected in His movements by the walls of a building or other such material obstruction, but comes and goes at will. The arrangement of the linen cloths in the tomb, as marked so keenly by Peter and John, is significant. They are found lying as they were when enfolding that body, as though He had in rising risen up through them.

Clearly the body is the same so far as personal identity is concerned. But the limitations are gone. The control of spirit over body seems full, without any limitations. As one of us can, in spirit, be in a place far removed as quick as thought, so He seems to have been able to be actually, bodily, where He wanted to be as quickly. All the old powers remain. All the old limitations are gone, never to return. Jesus had moved over to the life side of death. He had gone down into death's domain, given it a death blow, and then risen up into a new Eden life, where neither sin nor death had power to touch. Those forty days were sample days of the new Eden life on earth.

Jesus has become the leader of a new sort of life lived on the earth, mingling in its activities, but free of its power, controlled from above. He asks everyone who will to come along after Him. We can, for He has. It is possible, because of Him. We may, for He asks us to. It is our privilege. Let us go.

The Ascension: Back Home Again Until

Tarry ye – go ye.

One day the disciples and followers of Jesus had met in Jerusalem, when Jesus Himself came again in their midst and talked with them quite a bit. He said particularly that they were not to leave Jerusalem, but wait there. In a few days the Holy Spirit would come upon them, and they were to wait until He came. Then He asked them to go with Him for a walk. And they walk together along those old Jerusalem streets, out the gate and off past Gethsemane toward the top of Olives over against Bethany. On the way they ask Him if it was His plan to set up the kingdom then. He turns their thought away from Palestine toward the world, away from times and seasons toward telling a race about Himself.

And now they are standing together on the Mount of Olives. There is Peter, the new man of rock, and John and James, the sons of thunder, and little Scotch Andrew, and the man in whom is no guile, and the others. But one's eyes quickly go by these to the Man in the centre of the group. These men stand gazing on that face, listening for His words. There is a consciousness that the goodbye word is about to be spoken. Yonder they can see the bit of a depression and the tops of some old trees. That is Gethsemane. And over beyond that is the city wall and the little knoll nearby outside. That is Calvary. With memories such as these suggest they listen with eyes as well as ears. "Ye shall receive power," the Master is saying, "and ye shall be My witnesses here in Jerusalem and in all Judea, your brothers, and in Samaria, the nearby people you don't like, and unto the uttermost part of the earth, everybody else." They are held by the words and by that face. Then He lifts up His hands in blessing upon them. And as they gaze they notice He is rising, His feet are off the earth, then higher and higher. Then a shining glory cloud sweeps down out of the blue, and now they see Him no more.

Coming again.

They continue gazing, held spellbound by the sight, thinking maybe they may get another look. Then two men in white apparel are in their midst and speak to them: "Men of Galilee, why do you stand gazing up into the heavens? This Jesus who was received up into heaven shall so come in like manner as ye beheld Him going into heaven." That word at once sends them back to the waiting-place of which the Master had spoken. From that time they never lost the upward glance, but they were ever absorbed in obeying the Master's command.

Jesus' ascension was a continuation of the resurrection movement. The resurrection was the beginning of the ascension. Having finished the task involved in dying, Jesus responded to the natural upward movement of His life. On His way up from the tomb to His Father's home and throne, He tarried awhile on the earth for the sake of these disciples and leaders, then yielded again to the upward movement. The two men in white apparel give the key to the ascension. Jesus will remain above until the next great step in the kingdom plan. Then He will return to carry out in full the Father's great love-plan for man and for the earth.

His last act with these men was conducting them to the Mount of Olives. That is ever to be the point of outlook for His follower. Yonder in full view is Gethsemane and Calvary. Following the line of His eyes and pointing finger, as the last word is spoken, leads us ever to the man nearest by, to the uttermost parts of the earth, and to all between. Following His disappearing figure keeps us ever looking upward to Himself and forward to His return.

STUDY NOTES

Analysis and references

The spirit-key to an understanding of God's Word is surrender of will and life to His mastery. "He that is willing to do His will, will know of the teaching." The mental key to a grasp of the contents of that Book is habitual broad reading. It cannot be too insistently insisted upon that wide reading from end to end of the Book, and from end to end of the year, is the simple essential to a clear understanding and a firm grasp of the Bible.

It is the only possible salvation from the piece-meal, microscopic study of sentences and verses that has been in common use clear out of all proportion. Such disproportionate study steals away very largely the historical setting, and the simple meaning in the mind of speaker and writer. Wide reading habitually indulged in should come first, and out of that will naturally grow the closer study. This is the true order.

In giving references, it is needful to mark particular verses. Yet this is to be regretted because of our inveterate habit of reading only the marked verses instead of getting the sweep of their connection. The connection is a very large part of the interpretation of any passage. The references here are meant to be indices to the whole passage in connection.

They are not meant to be full, but simply to start one going. They should be supplemented by others suggested by one's own reading, by marginal references (those of the American Revision are specially well selected), and by concordance and topical text-book. What a student digs out for himself is in a peculiar sense his own. It is woven into his fibre.

It helps make him the man he comes to be. Those who may want a course to follow rigidly without independent study will find these notes disappointing.

For those who want a daily scheme of study the allotment for the day can be by certain designated pages of reading with the corresponding paragraphs in the Study Notes. The paragraphing will be found to be in some measure, though not wholly, a sub-analysis. The American Revision is used here.

The purpose of Jesus.

The Purpose in The Coming of Jesus.

God Spelling Himself out in Jesus: change in the original language – bother in spelling Jesus out – sticklers for the old forms – Jesus' new spelling of old words.

Jesus is God following us up: God heart-broken – man's native air – bad choice affected man's will – the wrong lane – God following us up.

The Early Eden Picture, Genesis 1:26-31. 2:7-25: unfallen man – like God – the breath of God in man – a spirit, infinite, eternal – love – holy – wise –

sovereign over creation, Psalm 8:5-8 – in his own will – summary – God's thought for man.

Man's Bad Break, Genesis 3. the climax of opportunity – the tree of choice – the temptation – blended lies – the tempter's strategy – the choice made – the immediate result – safety in shame – the danger of staying in Eden – guarding man's home – the return, Rev. 2:7. 22:14, 2. John 10:10.

Outside the Eden Gate: a costly meal – result in the man himself – ears and eyes affected – looking without seeing – a personal test – Isaiah's famous passage, Isaiah 6:9-10, see Isaiah 42:18, 20, 23. 43:8. 29:10. Jeremiah 5:21. 6:10. 7:26. Ezekiel 12:2. Psalm 69:23. Micah 3:6. Acts 7:51. – Jesus' use of parables – Jesus' irony – Matthew 13:10-15. Mark 4:10-12. Luke 8:9-10. See John 12:40. Acts 28:26, 27. Romans 11:8. John 9:39-41 – tongue affected – the tongue man's index – effect of seeing God – whole mental process affected – sense of dread – - Paul's seven steps down in mental process, Ephesians 4:17-19 – Jesus the music of God, the face of God.

Sin's Brood: result in the growth of sin – three stages, flood, Moses, Paul – Paul's Summary, Romans I:18-32, see Matthew 15:19. Galatians 5:19-21. 2 Timothy 3:2-5. – Paul's Outlook – a summary of to-day – the conventional cloak – four great paragraphs – man still a king, Genesis 9:6. 1 Corinthians 11:7. James 3:9. – a composite picture – analysis of sin – the root of sin.

God's Treatment of Sin: "gave them up," Romans 1:24, 26, 28. see Job 8:4. 1 Kings 14:16. Psalms 81:12. Acts 7:42, Romans 9:22 (endured). – the worst thing and the best – sin's gait – Jesus is God letting sin do its worst upon Himself.

A Bright Gleam of Light: the non-Christian world – God has no favourites – all know God directly, Romans 1:20, 32. John 1:9 – believing on Jesus – the outside majority – Peter's statement, Acts 10:34, 35. – Paul's statement, Romans 2:7. – persistent climbers – trusting the unknown Jesus – the Master's command – to help our brothers – Jesus is God sacrificing His best.

The Broken Tryst, Genesis 3:8-9: God keeping tryst – man not there – God's search – a lonely God – still calling – Jesus is God calling man back to the broken tryst.

God's Wooing: direct revelation to all – the inner light, John 1:9. Acts 17:26-28. Job 12:10. Psalms 139:1-16. – through nature, Psalms 19:1-6. – in the daily weave of life, Acts 17:28. – "The Lord's at the loom" – a special revelation, Romans 3:2. Deuteronomy 4:8. – in Jesus, Heb. 1:1-3. – the Book – the mission of the Book, John 20:31. – summary – chiefly Jesus.

The Plan for The Coming of Jesus.

God's Darling, Psalms 8:5-8. – the plan for the new man – the Hebrew picture by itself – difference between God's plan and actual events – one purpose through breaking plans – the original plan – a starting point – getting inside.

Fastening a Tether inside: the longest way around – the pedigree – the start.

First Touches on the Canvas: the first touch, Genesis 3:15. – three groups of prediction – first group: to Abraham, Genesis 12:1-3; to Isaac, Genesis 26:1-5; to Jacob, Genesis 28:10-15; through Jacob, Genesis 49:9-11. through Balaam, Numbers 24:17-19; through Moses, Deuteronomy 18:15-19, see Matthew 21:11. John 1:21. 6:14. Acts 3:22. 7:37. – second group: David, 2 Samuel 7:16, 18, 19. 23:3-5. Psalms 2nd, 110th. Solomon in 72nd Psalm. Forty-fifth Psalm.

A Full Length Picture in Colors: third group in prophetic books – one continuous subject – "day of the Lord," 134 times, – Somebody coming – His Person; divine, Isaiah 7:14. 9:6. 33:22. Micah 4:7. 5:2. Haggai 2:9. human, Isaiah 32:2. Daniel 7:13. manner of birth, Isaiah 7:14. of native stock, Isaiah 9:6. Ezekiel 29:21. of David's line, Isaiah 9:7. 11:1. 16:5. Jeremiah 23:5. 33:15, 17, 21, 26. Amos 9:11. Zechariah 3:8. 6:12. a branch of Jehovah, Isaiah 4:2. a King, Isaiah 9:6. 32:1. 33:17. Jeremiah 23:5. Zechariah 6:13. 9:9. called David, Jeremiah 30:9. Ezekiel 37:24, 25. Hosea 3:5. a priest-king, Zechariah 6:13. a preacher, Isaiah 61:1-3. a teacher, Isaiah 9:6 (counsellor). – the kingdom, Daniel 2:34,44. Obadiah:21 (Jehovah's). – the capital, Isaiah 2:3. 4:5. 33:20,21. 59:20. 65:18, 19. Joel 3:16, 17, 20, 21. Micah 4:7, 8. – the presence of God, Ezekiel 37:27. Joel 3:21. Zechariah 2:10, 11. Zephaniah 3:17. – visibly present, Isaiah 4:5, 6. – characteristics, vengeance, Isaiah 61:2. 63:1-6. Zephaniah 3:19. – great victory, Zechariah 9:9. – - but without force, Isaiah 11:4. Zechariah 9:10. – peace, Isaiah 2:4. 9:6, 7. – established in loving kindness, Isaiah 16:5. – justice and right, Isaiah 9:7. 16:5. 32:1. Jeremiah 23:5. 33:15. – the poor and meek, Isaiah 11:4, 5. – broken-hearted, poor and imprisoned, Isaiah 61:1-3. – protection from all ills, Isaiah 32:2. – impartiality in judging even the weakest and obnoxious, Isaiah 42:3, 4. – gradual increase, Isaiah 9:7. 42:4. a great crisis, Zephaniah 4:1. Habakkuk 3:1-15. with unexpected suddenness, Malachi

3:1 – effect upon Israel nationally; Spirit-baptized, Isaiah 44:2. Ezekiel 37:9-14. 39:29. – never withdrawn, Isaiah 59:21. – judgments removed, Zephaniah 3:14, 15. – impurity cleansed, Isaiah 4:4. Malachi 3:2, 3. – possession of land, Zephaniah 2:7. – capital holy, Joel 3:17. – weakness gone, Micah 4:6, 7. freedom from enemies, Isaiah 33:18, 19. – Jeremiah 30:8-10. Joel 3:17. Zechariah 14:11. Micah 5:6. – at peace, Isaiah 33:20. Micah 5:5. – leadership, Isaiah 2:2. Micah 4:1, 3. 5:8. – spiritual leadership, Joel 2:28, 29. – supremacy, etc., Isaiah 60:1-22. 11:10. 2:2. Micah 4:1, 3. 5:8. Zechariah 2:10. – Jerusalem centre, Isaiah 60:10-14. Zechariah 14:16. effect upon Israel personally; made over new, Ezekiel 11:17-20. 36:25-27. Jeremiah 31:31-34. Isaiah 4:3. – devotion and open-mindedness, Isaiah 32:3-4. 44:5. – sickness absent, Isaiah 33:24. – longer lives, Isaiah 65:20. – increase in numbers, Jeremiah 33:22. Ezekiel 37:26. Isaiah 44:4. – no disappointed plans, Isaiah 65:21-23. Amos 9:14. – fear gone, Micah 4:4. – thrilled hearts, Isaiah 60:5. effect upon other nations; to come back to God, Micah 5:3 (see John 10:16). – Spirit upon all, Joel 2:28. – voluntary coming to Israel for instruction, Isaiah 2:3. Micah 4:2. – earth filled with knowledge, Isaiah 11:9. – her influence as the dew, Micah 5:7. – the only medium, Isaiah 60:12. wondrous blessings shared with all, Isaiah 42:1, 6, 7. 49:6. 51:4. 61:1. – universal peace, Micah 4:3-4. Zechariah 9:10. changes in nature; at Jerusalem, Isaiah 33:21. Joel 3:18 l.c. Zechariah 14:8. Ezekiel 47:1-5. Zechariah 14:4. – increased light, Isaiah 30:26. – overshadowed by presence of God, Isaiah 60:19 (Presence cloud, Exodus; as sun, Matthew 17:2 with parallels; above sun Acts 26:13). – renewed fertility, Ezekiel 36:29, 30. Hosea 2:21. Joel 3:18. Amos 9:13. Zechariah 14:10. Isaiah 4:2. – removal of curse upon earth, Zechariah 14:11. Isaiah 65:17. – the animal creation, Isaiah 11:6-9. 65:25. Hosea 2:18 (see Romans 8:20-22). – without limit, Isaiah 2:2. 9:7. Daniel 2:44. 7:14. Micah 4:1. 5:4. Zephaniah 3:20. Zechariah 9:10. Joel 3:20. – a return to original conditions – characteristics of the coming One – mental equipment, Isaiah 11:2. 42:1. 61:1. – personal beauty and dignity, Isaiah 4:2. 33:17. Daniel 7:14. Micah 5:14. – unpretentious, Zechariah 9:9. – direct touch with God, Isaiah 49:1-3. 50:4. – backed by power of God, etc., Isaiah 42:1, 6. 49:3. 52:13. 53:11. 59:20. Zechariah 3:8. Malachi 3:1. – the poor cared for righteously, Isaiah 11:3-5. – divine insight, Isaiah 11:3.

Back to Eden: a wild dream – the Hebrew Book's conception – Simeon and Anna, Luke 2:25-38.

Strange Dark Shadowings: weird forebodings – acted out, Joseph and David – Psalms 22. 69:20, 21. Isaiah 50:6, 7. 52:13-53:12. Daniel 9:24-26. Zechariah 11:4-14. 12:10. 13:7. a valley-road to the throne.

The Tragic Break in The Plan.

The Jerusalem Climate: the contrasting receptions, Luke 2. the music of heaven, Job 38:6, 7. Luke 2:13, 14. pick out the choruses of Revelation, the crowning book. – the after-captivity leaders, see Ezra and Nehemiah – ideals and ideas – present leaders – Herod – the high priest – the faithful few, Luke 2:25, 38. 23:51.

The Bethlehem Fog: Matthew 1 and 2. Luke 2. a foggy shadow – suspicion of Mary – a stable cradle – murder of babes – star-students – senate meeting – a troubled city-flight – Galilee.

The Man Sent Ahead: the growing boy – John's relation to Jesus – trace passages in gospels referring to John.

The Contemptuous Rejection: accepted by individuals, rejected by nation – John's drawing power – a dramatic presentation. John 1:19-34. – ominous silence – five satisfied seekers, John 1:35-51. – cleansing of temple, John 2:13-22. – first public work, John 2:23-25. – Nicodemus, John 3:1-21. – helping John, John 3:22, 23. 4:1 with Matthew 3:5-7. Luke 3:7-14. the dispute about the two men, John 3:25-30 (note American Revision) – John's arrest – effect upon Jesus, Matthew 4:12-25. – "withdrew."

The Aggressive Rejection: the second stage – Nazareth, Luke 4:16-30. – seven incidents, i.e. (i) healing at pool of Bethesda, John 5:1-47. (2) forgiving and healing palsied man, Matthew 9:2-8 with parallels. (3) criticizing Jesus' personal conduct, Matthew 9:10-17 with parallels. (4) grain fields on the Sabbath, Matthew 12:1-8 with parallels. (5) healing whithered hand, Matthew 12:9-14 with parallels. – second "withdrew," Mark 3:7-12 with parallels. (6) charge of having an unclean spirit, Mark 3:20-30 with parallels. (7) interruption by his mother, Matthew 12:46-50 with parallels. – the murder of John, Matthew 14:1-12 with parallels. – third "withdrew," Matthew 14:13 with parallels. – staying in Galilee during fourth Passover, John 6:4, 5.

The Murderous Rejection: a fugitive from Judea, John 7:1. – fresh attack by southern leaders, Matthew 15:1-20 with parallel in Mark. – fourth "withdrew" – outside national lines, Matthew, 15:21 with parallel in Mark. – return to Sea of Galilee and request for sign, Matthew 15:29-16:4 with parallel in Mark. – Feast of Tabernacles, John 7: 2-8:59. – the blind man cured, John 9:1-40. – Transfiguration, Matthew 17:1-8 with parallels. – the beginning of the last journey, Luke 9:51. Mark 10:1, 32. Matthew 19:1. – the Seventy, Luke 10:1-17. – getting nearer to Jerusalem, divorce question, Mark 10:2-12. Matthew 19:3-12. – Good Samaritan, Luke 10:25-37. Beelzebub, "vehemently," Luke 11. fresh tilt over Sabbath question, Luke 13:10-17. – cunning attempt to get Him into Judea, Luke 13:31. – Feast of Dedication, John 10:22-40. – Lazarus, John 11:1-46. formal decision against Him, John 11:47-53. a fugitive, John 11:57. no more openly, John 11:54. crowding pilgrims, John 11:55, 56. Lazarus again, John 12:9-11. the last week; triumphal entry, Matthew 21:1-17 with parallels, daily visits and return to Olivet, Luke 21:37-38; cleansing temple, Matthew 21:12-17 with parallels; duel of questionings, Matthew 22. Mark 11:27-12:34. Luke 20:1-44; His terrific arraignment, Matthew 23:1-39 with parallels; Greeks, John 12:20-36. Bethany feast, Matthew 26:6-13 with parallels, Judas, Matthew 26:14-16 with parallels; with the inner circle, Matthew 26:17-46 with parallels.

Suffering the Birth-pains of a New Life: why did Jesus die? – God's plan of atonement, Leviticus 1:3-9 – Paul's statement in effect, Galatians 2:20. – Jesus' dying does not fit into Hebrew ritual – standpoint of Hebrews – what God counselled, Acts 2:23. – this affects only the form not the virtue of Jesus' death – preaching of Acts, 2:14-36, 38, 39. 3:12-26. 4:8-12. 5:29-32, and on, first church council, Acts 15.13-18 with Amos 9:11-12. – the superlative of hate – Jesus' death voluntary, John 10:17, 18 – ten attempts before the cross; three to kill at once, Luke 4:30. John 8:59. 10:31. other attempts, Matthew 12:14. John 5:18. 7:1, 30, 32. 10:39. 11:53 Jesus' own explanation: – the temple, John 2:19. lifted up, 3:15. Matthew 9:15 with parallels. His flesh, John 6:53-57. with Jesus' own interpretation, good Shepherd, John 10:11; for the sheep, 10:15; other sheep, 10:16; take it again, 10:17; of Myself, 10:18. cross, Matthew 10:38 with parallels. Jonah, Matthew 12:39, 40. 16:4 with parallel in Luke. Greeks, John 12:24-33. the Father's command, John 14:31. for friends, John 15:13. sanctified, John 17:19. the Father's cup, John 18:11. John's comment, John 12:47-52. – the necessity for dying – a step in a wider plan – for the nation – wholly voluntary – six elements in a perfect sacrifice – Jesus alone is a perfect sacrifice – Paul's comment, Romans 3:26. – God's master-stroke – faith – Hebrew heathen and Christian grouped.

Some Surprising Results of The Break.

The Surprised Jew: a clash of wills – thousands of believing Jews – the church displacing kingdom – two-fold division of men formerly – now three-fold – church different in organization from kingdom – the Baptist puzzled – Jesus did not fill out Hebrew prophecy – two characteristics, personal and official – personal details fulfilled – official not because of rejection – out of situation grew four gospels – Mark – Matthew's the gap gospel – Paul's audiences – Luke's gospel – these three tell of rejection mainly – John's gospel – the order of the gospels in canon.

The Surprised Church: God holds to His plan – mixed ideas of kingdom and church – a handy principle of interpretation – one law consistently applied – the church to fulfil its mission and go – the kingdom simply retarded, yet to come – the plan enriched – sliding scale of fulfilment – the King must come – - even this in Hebrew picture, Zechariah 12:10. New Testament teaching. Peter, Acts 3:21. – keeping truth in proportion – the gospel of the kingdom – Paul, 1 Thessalonians 1.10. 2:19. 3:13. 4:13-18. 5:10-23. 2 Thessalonians 1:7-10. 2:1-9. 1 Corinthians 1:7, 8. 3:13. 5:5. 15:23, 25, 51, 52. 16:22. 2 Corinthians 1:14. 5:2-4. Romans 8:18, 19, 23. 11:12-29. 13:11, 12. 16:20. Colossians 3:4. Ephesians 1:10, 14, 18. 4:4, 30. 5:27. Philippians 1:6, 10. 2:16. 3:20. 4:5. 1 Timothy 1:1 (note Paul's use of "hope" throughout). 6:14. Titus 2:13. 2 Timothy 1:12, 18. 2:12. 4:1, 8. – The Book of Revelation – the coming surprise. The Surprising Jew: greatest surprise – for all – the puzzle of history – divinely preserved – the keystone of the coming kingdom – Jesus the spirit magnet for Jew and all.

The person of Jesus.

The Human Jesus.

God's meaning of "Human": man's fellow – two meanings of word human – original meaning – natural limitations.

The Hurt of sin: sin's added limitations.

Our Fellow: Jesus truly human – up to first standard – His insistence – perfect in His humanness – fellowship in sin's limitations – hungry, Matthew 16:5. John 4:6-8. – tired, John 4:6. Mark 4:38. – poverty, Matthew 13:55. Mark 6:3. – hard toil, John 19:25-27. – homeless, Luke 4:16-30. Matthew 8:20. Luke 9:58. – discipline of waiting.

There's More of God since Jesus Went Back: the Nazareth home – fellowship with His brothers – "In the shop of Nazareth" – a Man on the throne.

The Divine Jesus.

Jehovah-Jesus: John 1:1-18. the intimacy of John, John 13:23. 19:26. 20:2. 21:7, 20. "with Jesus," John 18:15. – John writes of Jesus – – when he wrote – getting the range – his literary style – the beginning – the Word – this was Jesus – the tragic tone.

God's Spokesman: the Creator was Jehovah – – Jehovah is Jesus – the Spokesman – Old Testament revelations, Adam, Enoch, Noah, Abraham, Isaac, Jacob, Moses, the elders of Israel, Isaiah, Ezekiel, – Whom these saw – various ways of speaking – John's Gospel a battlefield – finding the Man. Whom Moses Saw: Jesus' own standpoint – "down from heaven," John 3:13, 31. 6:38. 8:42. would go back again, John 6:62. John 16:5, 10. 13:1. come on an errand, then going back, John 16:28 13:3. He only had seen the Father, John 6:46. only begotten Son, John 3:16, 18. His own Father, John 5:17, 18. 10:32-33. 19:7. – Jesus' answer to Jews' objection, John 5:19-47. – "He wrote of Me," the true meaning – I and the Father one, John 10:30. – the Father in Me, John 10:38. the name Father in Old Testament, 2 Samuel 7:14. 1 Chronicles 17:13. 22:10. Psalm 68:5. 89:26. 103:13. Isaiah 63:16. 64:8. Jeremiah 3:4, 19. Malachi 3:17. – Jehovah the common name – trace Jesus' use of Father about 180 times – manna, John 6:32.

Jesus is God Wooing Man: "Abraham – saw and was glad," John 8:33-59 – supposed meanings – natural meaning – "I am" – Jesus is Jehovah come Himself to woo man.

The Winsome Jesus.

The Face of Jesus: Jesus drew crowds, men, women, children, bad people, enemies – His personality – face – impress of experiences – the glory of God in that face, 2 Corinthians 4:6. Hebrews 1:3.

The Music of God in the Voice of Jesus: the eye – Jesus' eyes, Luke 4:16-30. John 8:59. 10:31. 7:32, 45, 46. 18:6. Mark 10:32. 9:36. 10:13-16. Luke 19:48. – His voice, Matthew 26:30. personal touch, Matthew 8:3, 15. 9:29. 17:7. 20:34. Mark 1:41. 7:33. Luke 5:13. 22:51. (John 14:16-20). His presence irresistible. Moses' request, Exodus 33:18. Jesus draws men – yielding to His power.

The great experiences of Jesus' life.

The Jordan: The Decisive Start.

MATTHEW 3:13-17. MARK 1:9-11. LUKE 3:21-22.

The Anvil of Experience: knowledge only through experience – the Fourth, Daniel 3:25. – three Hebrews, Daniel 3. – Babylonian premier, Daniel 6:16-23. – George Mueller – Jesus made perfect through experience, Hebrews 2:10. 5:8, 9. 7:28, l.c. – all our experiences, Hebrews 2:14-18. Philippians 2:7. Hebrews 4:15, except through sin, Hebrews 4:15, l.c. 7:26. 2 Corinthians 5:21, f.c. 1 Peter 2:22. 1 John 3:5, l.c. – Jesus' suffering, Philippians 2:6-8. Hebrews 2:9, 17, 18. 4:15. His obedience, Luke 2:51. Matthew 26:39. John 10:18. 14:31. Philippians 2:8. Romans 5:19. Hebrews 5:8. knowledge through experience – common experiences – mountain peaks – the tragic in each.

Our Brother: Jesus coming for baptism – John's objection – why baptized – getting in touch – the point of contact – choosing for Himself the Father's choice – the dangers – His strong purpose – the Father's approval – three times the voice, here, transfiguration, Matthew 17:5. Mark 9:7. Luke 9:35. Greeks, John 12:28. the decisive start.

The Wilderness: Temptation.

MATTHEW 4:1-11. MARK 1:12, 13. LUKE 4:1-13.

The University of Arabia: Jesus' naturalness – the Spirit's presence – intensity, Luke 2:45-51. – a true perspective – - the temptation's path – sin's path – John's grouping, 1 John 2:16. – the Spirit's plan – why – the devil's weakness – the Spirit's leading – a wilderness for every God-used man, Moses, Elijah, Paul.

Earth's Ugliest, Deepest Scar: Jesus the only one led up to be tempted – the wilderness – its history, Genesis 13:10-13. 18:16-19:38. – Jesus really tempted – no wrong here in inner response – every temptation – by the devil.

Waiting the Father's Word: the tempter's skill – acting divinely – a stone for hunger – not wrong in itself – recognizing temptation – "man" – waiting the Father's word – the trained inner ear – not our power but God's through our obedience.

Love never tests: a more agreeable setting – touching tender chords – the religious temptation – only through consent – bad scripture quoting, Psalm 91 – a helpful dust-cloth – using power only to help – a true quotation, Deuteronomy 6:16.

The Devil acknowledges the King: a dazzling scene – analysing the tempter's proposition – a common cunning trap – Jesus' kingly conduct – the devil obeys Him – but to return – a coward – our safety in Jesus – lead us not into temptation.

The Transfiguration: An Emergency Measure.

MATTHEW 16:28-17:1-8. MARK 9:1-8. LUKE 9:27-36.

God in Sore Straits: the darkest hour save one, fugitive, John 7:1. ban, John 9:22, 34. pushing, Matthew 15:1. Mark 7:1. – the danger zone, "withdrew," Matthew 4:12. 12:15. 14:13. 15:21. Tabernacles, John 7:32. 8:59. – Galileans desert, John 6:60-66. – the inner circle infected, John 6:67-71. – God needs men.

Fire and anvil for Leaders: mental strength – seasoned leadership – Simon and Peter.

An Irresistible Plan: alone with the twelve – the changed plan, Matthew 16:18-21. – Peter's stupid boldness, Matthew 16:22, with Mark 8:32. – the best available stuff – to see the Jesus within – getting Paul, Acts 9:1-9. 22:6-11. 26:12-18.

The Glory of that Light: while praying – changed from within – absorbed with Jesus' master-stroke – the jarring human note – the glory obscured – through an opened door – the kingdom.

A Vision of Jesus: gleams of light – the purpose secured, John 20:19, 24, 26-29. – an indelible impress, John 1:14. 12:41. Mark 9:3 with 1 Peter 1:16-17. Acts 12:2. – changed while looking, Acts 22:11. 2 Corinthians 3:18.

Gethsemane: The Strange, Lone Struggle.

MATTHEW 26:36-46. MARK 14:32-42. LUKE 22:39-46. HEBREWS 5:7.

The Pathway in: messengers ahead – Jesus felt the cross drawing near – the look of His face, Luke 9:51-55. – His disciples afraid, Mark 10:32. – indignation against sin, John 11:33, 38, marginal reading American Revision. – the Greeks, John 12:20-28.

The Climax of Suffering: the darkest shadow – why the struggle is strange – shock of extremes – His purpose in yielding – separation from the Father – Matthew 27:46. Mark 15:34 margin. – the superlative degree of suffering.

Alone: a full evening, Matthew 26:17-19 with parallels. John, chapters 13 to 17. – for prayer – on knees and face – the changed prayer – ready for the worst.

Calvary: Victory.

MATTHEW 26:47-27:61. MARK 14: 43-15:47. LUKE 22:47-23:56. JOHN 18:1-19:42.

Yielding to Arrest: the betrayal – protecting the disciples – checking Peter's violence – the arrest – the disciples forsake Him – except two, John 18:15, 16.

The Real Jewish Ruler: Annas the intriguer – an unrebuked insult – the case settled at once – before Caiaphas – difficulty in fixing a charge – the dramatic question and solemn answer – second condemnation – gross insults.

Held Steady by Great Love: Peter gains entrance through John, John 18:16. – the stammering denial – the bolder – with oaths and curses – Jesus' look – Peter's tears.

An Obstinate Roman: before the senate – trying to make a case – the formal condemnation – before Pilate – an unexpected set-back – alone with Pilate – acquitted – shrill protests – off to Herod.

A Savage Duel: before Herod – no word for him – more insults – a second acquittal – back to Pilate – his character – his summing up – their protests – his wife's message – Barabbas or Jesus – Pilate weakening – the scourging and coarse mocking – Pilate's surprise – a new charge – the governor startled – alone again with Pilate – the use of Caesar's name – renunciation of national hopes – the defeated governor's small revenge – the duel over.

Victory: out to Calvary – the pitying women – crucified – praying for the soldiers – pitching dice for His clothes – the inscription – coarse taunts and jests – winning a man at the very last – providing for His mother the darkness – the agonizing cry – the shout of victory.

The Resurrection: Gravity Upward.

MATTHEW 28:1-15. MARK 16:1-8. LUKE 24:1-49. JOHN 20:1-21:25. 1 CORINTHIANS 15:4-7.

A New Morning: early visit to the tomb – Mary Magdalene's alarmed call for Peter – the message of the angels – Peter and John come – another group of women get an angelic message.

Jesus seeking out Peter: Mary Magdalene meets Jesus – He meets other women – the soldiers' story – alone with Peter.

Made Known in the Breaking of Bread: the Emmaus travellers – the Stranger's explanation – the evening meal – the Master!

Even so Send I you: the meeting in Jerusalem – the Master's unexpected presence – the sure proofs – breathing on them – Thomas' stubborn doubts – a week later – a second great catch of fish – to James – to five hundred – on Olives' top – the Bethany home not represented.

Gravity Upward: the resurrection not expected – fully assured – the new victory-day – Jesus was raised – He rose at will – His dying voluntary, so the rising – man's true gravity – sin's gravity – Jesus' gravity upward.

The Life Side of Death: bodily changes in Jesus – personal identity unchanged – limitations gone – the Leader of a new sort of life.

The Ascension: Back Home Again Until…

Tarry ye – Go ye: The Jerusalem meeting – the walk to Olives – not Palestine only, but a world – the last word – upward – seen no more.

Coming again: gazing upward, Acts 1:10, 11. – a continuation upward – the Olivet outlook.

Also by Parvus Magna Press

Foundations of Faith for New Believers – Leaders Manual

Foundations of Faith for new believers is a series of 10 Bible Studies around the basics of the Christian faith. The 10 subjects including Faith, Salvation and Prayer are easy to understand simple Bible studies that encourage the new Christian in their faith and encourage them to ask questions about their walk with God.

The Foundations of Faith series has sold over 30,000 copies since it was first published about 15 years ago and has helped thousands of new believers become valuable members of the congregation.

This is the Leaders Manual which has plenty of space for notes and comments for the study leader and you can also get a student's manual.

Paperback ISBN 978-1910372005

Kindle ISBN 978-1910372067

Foundations of Faith for New Believers – Students Manual

This is the Student Manual which is a great give-away, either at the start of the course or at the end as a prize for further study. All of the material contained in the leader's manual is here for the students.

Paperback ISBN 978-1910372012

Also in the Evangelical Heritage Library

We have modernised the language of all these classic books, without losing the essential spirit and tone of the original work. We have also added many footnotes to explain cultural and social references that may not necessarily be known to the modern reader.

James Black – The Mystery of Preaching

In this incredible work James Black looks deeply into the art and science of preaching. He teaches the skills needed to construct deep and relevant sermons that excite and move the congregation and "prepare them for every good work".

This book is a must read for the new pastor as well as those older and well – experienced workmen – even if it's just as a reminder!

ISBN: 978-1-910372-07-4 Paperback
ISBN: 978-1-910372-08-1 Paperback
ISBN 978-1-910372-09-8 Kindle/Kobo

James Black – Around the Guns

James Black manages to communicate the gospel with a clarity and fervour that are infectious and although his illustrations and stories may seem at first to be dated and without application in this modern computerised world, the underlying message comes through loud and clear.

I enjoyed transcribing this book thoroughly and more than once found my prayer closet to deal with issues in my own heart that I felt I had already dealt with years ago.

I hope this volume blesses you and your ministry just as it has blessed mine.

ISBN 978-1-910372-10-4 Paperback
ISBN 978-1-910372-11-1 Paperback
ISBN 978-1-910372-12-8 eBook

www.ingramcontent.com/pod-product-compliance
Lightning Source LLC
LaVergne TN
LVHW061223060426
835509LV00012B/1403